BEDSIDE BOOK
OF BRIDGE

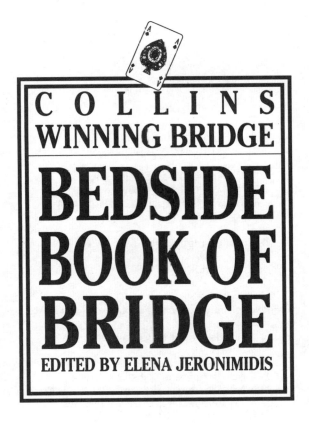

COLLINS
WINNING BRIDGE

BEDSIDE
BOOK OF
BRIDGE

EDITED BY ELENA JERONIMIDIS

CollinsWillow
An Imprint of HarperCollins*Publishers*

First published in 1993 by
Collins Willow
an imprint of HarperCollins*Publishers*
London

© Elena Jeronimidis and *BRIDGE PLUS* 1993

ISBN 0 00 218451 6

Front cover playing cards supplied by John Beard

Illustrations by Celia Weber

Text snippets in tinted boxes reproduced
by permission of *BRIDGE PLUS*
pp 36 and 148: Articles reprinted from *1994 Collins Bridge Diary*
p 96: Bridge hand from *Moonraker* by Ian Fleming reproduced
by permission of Glidrose Publications
p 162: Quotation from 'Blood Pressure' in omnibus edition of
On Broadway by D Runyon reproduced by permission
of Constable Publishers

Printed and bound in Great Britain by
Cox & Wyman Ltd

CONTENTS

CONTENTS

ACKNOWLEDGEMENTS

This book could not have been published without the help and co-operation of all its contributors, and the Editor wishes to acknowledge the fundamental part which they – and their enthusiasm – played in the production of the *Bedside Book of Bridge*.

Thanks are also due to Eric Crowhurst for checking the technical content; Roger Trowell, Dennis Cook and Bernard Magee for reading the manuscript; John Magee for many useful suggestions; and especially Andrew Parker for much constructive criticism.

INTRODUCTION

BY ELENA JERONIMIDIS

One of the articles in this book describes bridge as the only game in which complete beginners may find themselves competing against world champions. This is indeed one of the charms of bridge, which the *Bedside Book of Bridge* mirrors by bringing together world-famous bridge personalities and ordinary players, professionals and amateurs alike.

Only very few of the articles contained in the *Bedside Book of Bridge* have already been published elsewhere. They are reprinted here either because they represent the best of an individual author, or because their contents seemed particularly appropriate to the spirit of this anthology. The overwhelming majority of the articles included, however, have been written especially for the *Bedside Book of Bridge* by contributors from all over the world.

This is, of course, the other beauty of bridge: wherever you are, there will be a game available – and with it a passport to friendship. Indeed many players care less for the intellectual challenges of bridge than its social dimension, and this approach to the game has to be recognized and valued. Equally, it can be very rewarding to explore what may, at first glance, appear peripheral to bridge: that is, the humorous situations which the game generates, the types of player it attracts – not to mention its history and its curios.

The *Bedside Book of Bridge* illustrates all aspects of bridge under several headings: 'Tournament Bridge' describes some of the best (and the worst!) of high-level duplicate play; 'Better Bridge' will help improvers and average players alike to sharpen their game; and our 'Bridge Puzzles' will keep you awake for hours, and fill you with frustration (or satisfaction). If it is entertainment you are after, turn to 'Bridge Fiction' or to 'It Happened One Night' – which proves that nothing is as large as life. 'Holiday Bridge' and 'Bridge-à-Brac' complete our selection, the former intended to explore a new area of the game which is becoming increasingly popular, the latter to bring together all the information, oddities, and feelings that add so much to our enjoyment of bridge. If that's not enough, the snippets sprinkled here and there might raise a chuckle – and give you a better understanding of the lore and language of bridge.

The challenge of every anthology is that it has to cater for a variety of tastes and interests. A bridge anthology must also take into account the fact that no two players hold identical views – and everybody thinks they're right. As long as you are not afraid to smile, this is the book for you.

FEARFUL SYMMETRY

BY DAVE HUGGETT

Dummies which have the same distribution as the closed hand are always tedious because they offer no immediate scope for scoring ruffs, but they can be interesting in their own way.

South had one such dummy in the deal that follows – although his immediate concern was to berate partner for underbidding.

♠ A 8 7 6 2
♡ A 7
♢ K 9 6 2
♣ K 2

How would you have played 6♠ on the ♠Q lead? Trumps break 3–0.

```
        N
  W         E
        S
```

♠ K 9 5 4 3
♡ K 6
♢ A Q 7 4
♣ A 4

Solution on page 210.

THE ADVANTAGES OF AGE

Two Junior Camrose triallists sat North–South at their local club. West, dealer, passed at Love All; North opened 1♣, East overcalled a pre-emptive 3♠ and eventually South played in 4♡.

North was not pleased with the result, and the traveller confirmed that a cold slam in any denomination had been missed – couldn't South bid more energetically on his 18-count, and ignore a facetious overcall based on a 3-count? South said ruefully: 'I thought she was too old to bid on tram tickets!'

East – a lady in her early forties – thought to herself that age has its own compensations.

THE ABBOT MOVES WITH THE TIMES

BY DAVID BIRD

'One diamond', said Brother Paulo.

The Abbot, next to speak, thumbed through his cards uncertainly:

♠ A Q 10 8 3
♡ A J 4
◇ K 6
♣ 9 7 3

Fourteen points, what should he do? Should he double, to get the strength over, or start with 1♠? The modern idea seemed to be to make the suit overcall. If Left-Hand Opponent competed with 2◇ and this ran back to him, he could make a take-out double on the second round. 'One spade', said the Abbot.

The opponents, paying little attention to this carefully considered intervention, bid promptly to 3NT. This was the complete deal:

Dealer: North
Love All

			♠ 7 5
			♡ K 5
			◇ A Q 8 5 2
			♣ K 10 8 4

♠ 9 4	N	♠ A Q 10 8 3
♡ Q 9 8 7 6 2	W E	♡ A J 4
◇ J 9 7 3		◇ K 6
♣ 5	S	♣ 9 7 3

			♠ K J 6 2
			♡ 10 3
			◇ 10 4
			♣ A Q J 6 2

South	West	North	East
Brother	Brother	Brother	The
Lucius	Xavier	Paulo	Abbot
		1◇	1♠
2♣	NB	3♣	NB
3NT	End		

The ♠9 lead ran to declarer's Jack and the silver-haired Brother Lucius crossed to the ♣K to lead a second round of spades. The Abbot rose with the Ace and, for want of anything better to do, exited with the ♠Q. Brother

Lucius won in hand and cashed two more clubs, removing the Abbot's safe exit card. The following was the end position:

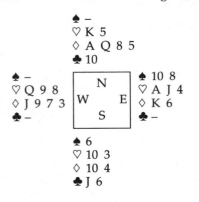

```
              ♠ –
              ♡ K 5
              ◇ A Q 8 5
              ♣ 10
♠ –                        ♠ 10 8
♡ Q 9 8      N             ♡ A J 4
◇ J 9 7 3  W   E           ◇ K 6
♣ –          S             ♣ –
              ♠ 6
              ♡ 10 3
              ◇ 10 4
              ♣ J 6
```

Lucius now exited with his last spade, throwing a diamond from dummy. The Abbot could cash one more spade, a further diamond being thrown from the table, but then had to concede a ninth trick in one of the red suits. He gave an exasperated shake of the head. 'Can't you lead a heart from six to the Queen?' he exclaimed. 'Isn't that obvious? We take the first seven tricks, then.'

'I would have led a heart if it wasn't for your overcall', replied Brother Xavier. 'You had fourteen points, didn't you? Isn't it better to start with a double on that type of hand?'

Brother Paulo, the Italian monk, leaned forward. 'Perhaps you would be reaching 4♡ after a double', he suggested. 'That needs a tight defending to beat it, I think. After a club lead you would have a good possibility to set up the spades.'

The Abbot gave an irritated flap of the hand. 'It's all completely irrelevant', he declared. 'Don't any of you read the magazines? *All* the top players overcall 1♠ on this type of hand nowadays, it's automatic.'

Brother Paulo nodded happily as he inspected the score-sheet. As expected, 3NT bid and made was a complete top. 'The other East players seem to be playing a sadly old-fashioned game tonight, Abbot', he observed. 'Perhaps they are not reading the right magazines.'

VIRTUE MUST BE ITS OWN REWARD

The Abbot reached piously for his score-card. 'Virtue must be its own reward on such hands', he said.

HONEYMOON BRIDGE

BY DAVID BURN

This is the story of one of the most memorable events of my honeymoon. No, it is not what you think – our wedding had been carefully planned so that we would spend our honeymoon in Ostend, playing in the European Mixed Bridge Championships. As all husbands will know, my part in the planning process had consisted of saying: (a) 'Yes, dear', when told what to do; and (b) 'No, dear', when told what not to do; and (c) 'Sorry, dear', when I had done something in category (b) – or when I had not heard my instructions. Su, my wife of four days, and I had reached the final of the Mixed Pairs Championship and were doing tolerably well when this deal occurred:

Dealer: North
Love All

	♠ A 8 6 4
	♡ A Q 3
	◇ J 2
	♣ K 9 6 5

♠ Q 10 5 2 ♠ J 7
♡ 10 8 5   ♡ J 9 7
◇ 8 7 6 5   ◇ A K Q 10 9 3
♣ 8 4   ♣ 7 2

♠ K 9 3
♡ K 6 4 2
◇ 4
♣ A Q J 10 3

South	West	North	East
David		Su	
		1NT	NB
2♣ (a)	NB	2♠	NB
3♣ (b)	NB	3♡ (c)	NB
3♠ (c)	NB	4♣	NB
4◇ (c)	NB	4♡ (c)	NB
6♣ (d)	End		

(a) Stayman.
(b) Natural, game-forcing.
(c) Cue-bids.
(d) Totally unwarranted!

We would have scored very well on this deal simply for staying out of 3NT, the optimum contract at pairs being 4♡. A 5♣ contract would have been plenty for a decent score, though – 6♣ looked like being a disaster, as there was no obvious way to avoid losing a spade and a diamond for one down. What was more, I could not even take refuge in the standard husband's tactics of blaming partner for her bidding, since Su's bids had all been very sound ones.

It seemed to me at the time – and it still does – that West was wrong not to lead a diamond, but perhaps my cue-bid in the suit put him off. At any rate, his actual choice of a heart meant that I had the slenderest of chances to make my contract. *All* I needed was for hearts to divide 3–3, trumps not to be worse than 3–1, and East to have not more than two spades and the ◇A–K–Q! As you can see from the diagram, this magic distribution was the one that actually existed, but those of you who have not seen it already may like to work out how I was able to make the contract.

I won the heart lead, drew trumps in two rounds, and cashed three more hearts discarding a diamond from the table. Next I played the ♠A–K before leading the ◇J in this position:

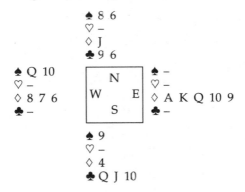

East had to win the diamond, and lead another round of the suit, so I was able to ruff in dummy and discard my losing spade.

Making 6♣ was a top – which proves that one can be lucky at cards without, as the proverb says, being unlucky in love.

UNUSUAL CONVENTIONS

'What's the range of your 1NT?'
'Variable. If we hold the cards in the left hand it's 12–14, if we hold them with the right it's 15–17.'

SIGNAL FAILURE

BY ERIC CROWHURST

If your partner leads the Ace against a suit contract, should you *always* start a peter if you hold
a small doubleton? Or should you play high-low
only if you want to ruff the third round? This is
obviously an important point, which should be
discussed by regular partnerships, for there will
otherwise be situations in which a dutiful peter
will attract an unwanted ruff. East believed that a
situation of that kind had arisen on this deal from
a recent match:

Dealer: North
Love All

```
                              ♠ K 7 4
                              ♡ A Q J 8 3
                              ◇ A 6 5
                              ♣ Q 4
         ♠ A 8              ┌─────────┐         ♠ Q J 3
         ♡ K 2             │    N    │         ♡ 10 9 7 6 4
         ◇ J 9 3           │ W     E │         ◇ 8 7 4
         ♣ A K 10 7 6 2    │    S    │         ♣ 9 5
                              └─────────┘
                              ♠ 10 9 6 5 2
                              ♡ 5
                              ◇ K Q 10 2
                              ♣ J 8 3
```

South	West	North	East
		1♡	NB
1♠	2♣	2♠	NB
NB	3♣	3♡	NB
3♠	End		

West cashed the ♣A–K against the final contract of 3♠, and East felt that
it would be misleading not to show his doubleton club. He therefore
signalled with ♣9–5, and West naturally continued with a third round
of clubs. Declarer discarded a diamond from dummy, and East ruffed
with some reluctance, bearing in mind that he was effectively ruffing
with his certain trump trick.

East switched to the ◇8 at trick four; South went up with the King,
and then led a small trump towards dummy. By this time, West had
realized that there were no more side-suit tricks available for the
defence. She therefore decided to play for the only remaining chance of

16

defeating the contract: a trump-promotion play. West rose majestically with the ♠A, noticing the fall of the ♠J from her partner, and fired back a fourth round of clubs. No matter whether or not South elected to ruff high in dummy, East's ♠Q was now certain to become the setting trick – and his unwanted ruff at trick three had been the vital move in defeating the contract.

East was certainly right to peter in diamonds on the following deal; it was at trick three that he went astray:

Dealer: South
E/W Vul

```
                                      ♠ Q J 4
                                      ♡ 8 5 2
                                      ◊ 7 5 4
                                      ♣ A K J 7
            ♠ 10 7 6 5      ┌─────────────┐   ♠ K 9 8 3 2
            ♡ –             │      N      │   ♡ K 10 9 7
            ◊ A K 8 6 3     │  W       E  │   ◊ 9 2
            ♣ 8 6 4 2       │      S      │   ♣ 5 3
                            └─────────────┘
```

South	West	North	East
1♡	NB	2♣	NB
3♡	NB	4♡	End

```
                                      ♠ A
                                      ♡ A Q J 6 4 3
                                      ◊ Q J 10
                                      ♣ Q 10 9
```

West began by leading the ◊A–K, on which East completed a heavy peter with the ◊9 and ◊2. West obediently played a third diamond, which was ruffed by East – but that was the end of the defence,

After ruffing the third diamond, East switched to a spade. South won with the ♠A and used the club entries to dummy to take two heart finesses and make his contract.

It seemed obvious for East to ruff declarer's diamond winner at trick three, but this was actually an error. If East discards a club on the third diamond, the contract will be defeated. South wins with the ◊Q, but he no longer has two club entries to dummy with which to take two heart finesses. He will therefore be compelled to lose two trump tricks to East, and concede a one-trick defeat.

It was not easy, but East should probably have found the winning defence. Since South has made a jump rebid without the ♣A–K, the ◊A–K, the ♠K, and the ♡K, he *must* have the ♠A. This means that East has to come to two trump tricks in order to defeat the contract, and he can ensure this by nullifying one of declarer's entries to dummy.

IF YOU CAN'T BEAT THEM, YOU CAN JOIN THEM

BY MARK HORTON

Tournament bridge allows players of every standard, from beginner to expert, to test their skill. Aside from the chance of winning, there are other hidden benefits. Imagine having taken your first golf lesson and then immediately finding yourself standing on the first tee with the world's No. 1, Nick Faldo – or perhaps you would like to play tennis against Monica Seles. Of course it won't happen, but in bridge it can. Wherever you play, you are likely to find a number of top-class players in every event, and you may get the chance to play against them.

The popularity of bridge means that you can travel all around the world to enjoy your favourite game. The biggest tournaments in terms of numbers are staged in North America. In April 1993 the Regional at Gatlinburg, Tennessee, attracted a record 5100 tables. Let's take a look at a defensive play from that event by one of the world's top women players, Sabine Zenkel. She represents Germany, but lives in Chicago. Try it first as a problem.

Dealer: North
Game All

♠ A Q 7 5
♡ A 2
◇ 8
♣ A Q J 9 5 2

South	West	North	East
		1♣	Dbl
2♡ (a)	3◇	3♡	End

```
            N        ♠ K J 9 3
        W       E    ♡ K Q 10 3
            S        ◇ K 7 4 3
                     ♣ 8
```

(a) Weak, standard treatment in America.

Partner leads the ◇Q. Declarer wins with the Ace, finesses the ♣J, and tries to cash the Ace. You ruff with the ♡3 while partner shows an even number of clubs. What do you do next? The full deal is shown at the top of page 19.

There is only one winning card: the ♡10. Declarer can win with the Jack, but must then lose one spade, two hearts and two diamonds or, if declarer takes a ruff with the ♡A, one spade, three hearts and one diamond. Did you, like Zenkel, work all that out?

18

```
              ♠ A Q 7 5
              ♡ A 2
              ◊ 8
              ♣ A Q J 9 5 2
♠ 10 8 4          N          ♠ K J 9 3
♡ 7                          ♡ K Q 10 3
◊ Q J 10 5 2   W     E       ◊ K 7 4 3
♣ K 10 7 6        S          ♣ 8
              ♠ 6 2
              ♡ J 9 8 6 5 4
              ◊ A 9 6
              ♣ 4 3
```

Whilst European tournaments cannot compete with the size of those staged in America they, unlike their American counterparts, often carry the incentive of valuable cash prizes. The best of these are staged in France and Holland, whilst Austria, Germany and Spain are not far behind. Great Britain offers tournaments which are well organized, but not well rewarded.

Of course, in all the major championships the players are in search of medals, not money. Great Britain's Sandra Landy has won a fair number of those over the years, and she captured a golden one in the Women's Teams at the 14th EC Championships. Here is a hand she played in that event:

```
Dealer: West   ♠ K J 4 2
N/S Vul        ♡ A 2
               ◊ A Q 6 5
               ♣ K 9 2
♠ 8 6             N          ♠ 10
♡ 10 9 8 7 4 3               ♡ K Q J
◊ 7 3          W     E       ◊ K 9 8 2
♣ 7 6 5           S          ♣ Q 10 8 4 3
               ♠ A Q 9 7 5 3
               ♡ 6 5
               ◊ J 10 4
               ♣ A J
```

Sandra was declarer in a contract of 6♠ from the South hand. West led a heart, so Sandra won, drew trumps, and led the ◊J.

When West did not produce the King, Sandra remembered the 'Bols Bridge Tip' (see pages 45–47) of the Pakistani expert Zia Mahmood ('If they don't cover, they don't have it!') and called for dummy's ◊A. Now a winning club finesse enabled her to dispose of her losing heart and simply concede a diamond.

She earned a slam swing for her side, because Israel were also in 6♠, but North was the declarer. With the ◊10 being visible, West was never going to cover the Jack, and declarer had no real reason not to rely on the diamond finesse.

You may not be able to play as well as Sabine and Sandra, but you can play against them!

CONFESSIONS OF A TOUR OPERATOR

BY MIKE SWANSON

At the start of December, when the winter is just beginning to bite, whenever you turn on commercial television, or open the newspaper, you suddenly find yourself being besieged with adverts for summer holidays. Bridge players suffer a similar experience, although recently it has become a year-round onslaught, with the English Bridge Union's magazine often looking more like a holiday brochure.

But how does a bridge holiday operator go about choosing destinations and hotels? Well, just like anybody else, we start by raiding our local travel agent's shelves. Ideally, what we are seeking is a large modern hotel (with a superb conference room) in an unspoilt area next to a deserted, golden, sandy beach, with plenty of local shops no more than a stroll away – and of course there must be direct daytime flights available from Gatwick, Birmingham, Manchester, and Glasgow, to an airport that is no more than forty minutes from the hotel. Oh, yes – and the price must be less than £600 for a two-week half-board package! Needless to say, I am still looking for that perfect venue, so if you come across anywhere that comes close, please drop me a line.

Eventually, after much heart-searching, we settle on a resort and a list of possible hotels – and then our problems begin! Apart from my long-since-forgotten schoolboy French, I speak no other language than English and, rather unreasonably, I expect hotel staff the world over to have a firm grasp of my native tongue. So, quite often it takes several phone calls and faxes before I manage to contact someone who can communicate with me, and then they have to struggle with a dictionary in order to send communications such as the following extracts:

We are felicitatious to welcome your group ... We can offer a confarance room with much lights ... All bedrooms have air candition and minihar ... We have many umberellas and deck charis by our pool.

I shouldn't really mock foreigners struggling with our language, since we have been known to offer such items as '*tin-bedded rooms*' and '*double births*' in our literature in the past!

Our next step is to visit the resort and its hotels. This is sometimes easier said than done, if we want to go outside of the normal tourist season. A recent trip to Turkey meant that we had to change aircraft in Istanbul. A coach took us all to the second aircraft, where we then waited on the tarmac for our luggage to arrive. Eventually a lorry arrived, and cases galore were taken off – none of which were claimed by those waiting. Two lorries later, our luggage turned up, leaving me with the image of lorries driving around the airport offering their cargo to any likely-looking crowd of people.

One aspect of looking at hotels, which always seems to leave the management with a perplexed look on their faces, is my insistence on measuring the dimensions of the conference room in pigeon

MEASURING THE DIMENSIONS OF THE CONFERENCE ROOM IN PIGEON STEPS

steps. I have discovered that size-nine shoes are almost exactly a foot long (excuse the pun), and I have learned to treat with a degree of scepticism the dimensions published in the hotel's literature.

So, at last the holiday is confirmed and advertised, bookings are taken, and the group is on its way. Nothing can go wrong, can it? I wish that were so. Playing-cards and stationery are very heavy, and despite advance notification of excess baggage the official on the check-in desk often denies all knowledge, and insists that some of my luggage must go on standby. I have to get my priorities right, so it is my clothes that suffer this fate – after all you can't play bridge without cards!

Finally we reach the hotel, and people settle in. Apart from the weather, our main worry is that our clients might not be able to cope with the lack of sophistication which they are bound to find in certain parts of the world. On a trip to a beautiful island in the Mediterranean, we had water dripping through one of the light fittings in the bridge room (it wasn't raining) and the hotel's solution was to place a dustbin under it for a whole fortnight!

Fortunately we are blessed with clients who retain both their patience and their sense of humour in such circumstances.

21

LITTLE CLUBLINGTON'S SILENT BIDDER

BY PETER STOCKEN

The Little-Clublington-by-the-Marsh Bridge Club was thriving: they played duplicate three nights a week, and rubber on Thursday afternoons; their membership was increasing; they had affiliated themselves to the English Bridge Union, and the competition was intense as to who would first reach the rank of County Master.

There was, however, one small cloud on the horizon: the bidding boards which had been purchased from the EBU. At the first AGM – held in the top room of the *George and Dragon* – members unanimously agreed that either the EBU played a completely different game from Little Clublington, or they had been sent the wrong boards. The Secretary was asked to check on the latter, while in the meantime the Treasurer, who had taught art at the local primary school prior to retiring, offered to design a bidding board more in tune with the needs of the club. What he produced (which was immediately adopted by the club) is shown opposite. Readers who have never played at Little Clublington may find the following glossary helpful:

1. Penalties! Leave it!
2. Take-out.
3. I'm not sure what it is, but I should have bid on the last round.
4. HELP!
5. We've got them!
6. A spade.
7. A trowel.
8. We're playing Precision, remember?
9. Strong hand, partner, so wake up.
10. Sort of strong hand, so keep going a bit longer.
11. Convention, partner.
12. This is the bid we discussed in the car on the way here and which I bet you've forgotten.
13. Prepared.
14. I have absolutely no interest in this hand!

15. 6–8 points.
16. 9–11 points.
17. I've got 12–14 points too!
18. I'm void in your suit.
19. I like your shape, partner.

It is rumoured that when one of these bidding boards – by a curious and devious route – reached the EBU's Laws & Ethics Committee, the Chairman of that august body fainted, and all attempts to revive him failed until someone had the bright idea of whispering into his left ear the cabalistic intonation 'Fielded Psyche'.

At the second AGM of the Little-Clublington-by-the Marsh BC, the Chairman said that he knew he was speaking on behalf of all members in congratulating the Treasurer for producing such an excellent piece of work. Later on in the meeting, the Secretary mentioned that whenever she rang the EBU the 'phone went dead; she had contacted British Telecom to check for faults on the line.

This article is reprinted by kind permission of BRIDGE PLUS.

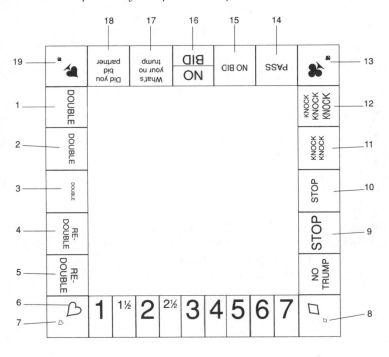

PROTECTION RACKET

BY PETER HAWKES

South
♠ K Q 10 7
♡ Q 9 4 3
◊ 10 9
♣ Q 8 2

What could be more boring than a flat nine-count on a Tuesday night at the club? I was the dealer at Love All. We were not playing a Mini No-trump, so I passed. The bidding went Pass, One No-trump, Pass, back to me. We were not playing a strong no-trump, so I passed and reached for my score-card. But wait – there were *five* more rounds of bidding in which I bid spades and hearts, *and* doubled the opponents in clubs, diamonds, and no-trumps! The full deal and bidding sequence are given below:

Dealer: South
Love All

```
                          ♠ A J 9 2
                          ♡ A K 10 7
                          ◊ 5 2
                          ♣ J 6 4
      ♠ 8 5 4 3                          ♠ 6
      ♡ 8 5 2            N               ♡ J 6
      ◊ A K 6 3      W        E          ◊ Q J 8 7 4
      ♣ K 5              S               ♣ A 10 9 7 3
                          ♠ K Q 10 7
                          ♡ Q 9 4 3
                          ◊ 10 9
                          ♣ Q 8 2
```

South	West	North	East
NB	NB	1NT	NB
NB	Dbl	NB	2♣
2♠	NB	NB	2NT
Dbl	NB	NB	3♣
Dbl	3◊	NB	NB
3♡	NB	NB	4◊
Dbl	End		

Minus 510 was not quite a bottom, since one pair was doubled in *three* diamonds. The deal was played ten times, five by East–West and five by North–South, in nine different contracts.

Maybe some flat nine-counts are less boring than others!

A MIRACLE CHANCE

BY ULRICH AUHAGEN

The ♡Q is led against South's contract of 7♠. Is there a chance of bringing home this silly Grand against best defence?

Solution on page 211.

♠ J
♡ K 7 4 3 2
◇ A Q
♣ A Q 6 5 3

```
        N
   W         E
        S
```

♠ A Q 6 5 4 3 2
♡ –
◇ K J 10 9
♣ K J

A DANGEROUS GAME

'Cards, or any kind of gaming, at all times the worst of amusements, should be particularly avoided during pregnancy. The temper is then more liable to be ruffled by the changes of luck and the mind to be fatigued by constant exertions of the judgement and memory. Old maids are the only class of females who may be allowed to spend some of their tedious hours in such absurd and such unhealthy pastimes.'

This extract (from a section on general rules of female conduct and moral habits in *The New Female Instructor: The Young Woman's Guide To Domestic Happiness*, an interesting publication which first appeared in the 1830s) was reprinted by the *Surrey CBA Bulletin* with the appropriate comment, 'Perhaps there is a case for a compulsory health warning to be printed on packs of playing cards!'

SENSE AND SENSIBILITY

BY QUEENIE PENGUIN

It was the qualifying heat for the National Pairs. To the organizers' regret, not many members of the Emperor Club had bothered to enter, even though the club itself was charging no table money for the event. The reason for this was that the weaker players objected to paying 450 Icicles to the Penguin Bridge Union for the privilege of being knocked out immediately, and not even Colonel Chinstrap – a pillar of the Emperor's committee and a staunch supporter of the PBU – had felt it appropriate to encourage fellow members to pay such an exorbitant sum.

As a result, only five tables were in play, made up of the club's top players and a few pairs whom the Colonel had roped in to boost the numbers and make the competition a bit less of a lottery.

One such pair was Elspeth and the Jackass, who – to their surprise – were having quite a good session, most of their results being above average with a few occasional tops thrown in by those opponents who had totally underestimated their current form. It was therefore with a warm feeling of optimism that they approached the table where a new, strong partnership was sitting North–South – the Little Blue Penguin and Archibald.

With so few tables in play, each round was of four boards, and this was the crucial one:

Dealer: North
E/W Vul

		♠ K J 10 8	
		♡ A J 10	
		◇ K 8 7 6 3	
		♣ 8	

♠ 7 4 2			♠ 9 6 3
♡ 3 2	W	N E	♡ Q 8 6 4
◇ J 9 5		S	◇ Q 10 2
♣ A K J 6 3			♣ Q 7 5

		♠ A Q 5
		♡ K 9 7 5
		◇ A 4
		♣ 10 9 4 2

South	West	North	East
Archibald	Jackass	Little Blue	Elspeth
		1◇	NB
1♡	NB	1♠	NB
2♣ (a)	NB	2♡	NB
4♡	End		

(a) Fourth Suit Forcing.

Against 4♡ by South, the Jackass led the ♣A and continued with the ♣K. Archibald gave the hand brief thought, then ruffed in dummy and played a diamond to his Ace. A third club was ruffed with the ♡J, the ◇K cashed, a diamond ruffed in hand, then three rounds of spades were played ending in dummy. This was the position when Archibald led dummy's last spade:

With only trumps left, Elspeth ruffed with the ♡4; Archibald over-ruffed with the ♡7, and the Jackass threw a club. Next the ♣10 was ruffed with dummy's ♡A (East underruffing), and a diamond was led: whichever trump East chose to ruff with, declarer would overruff and claim the rest of the tricks.

Seeing Elspeth's discomfiture. Archibald allowed himself a brief smile and tabled his hand: 'Twelve tricks', he announced with just the faintest trace of self-satisfaction in his voice.

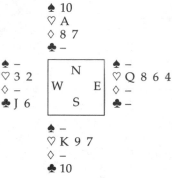

'Very elegant', drawled the Little Blue Penguin, to whom trump coups were routine, in a determined effort to keep on his partner's right side so that at the next Committee Meeting Archibald would support a motion that the restrictions imposed upon the Little Blue Penguin's membership should be removed, and he would no longer be obliged to partner only Colonel Chinstrap at the club's normal duplicate sessions. His somewhat sycophantic compliment, however, turned to genuine praise when he opened the traveller and entered plus 480 in the North–South column for a clear top – most Souths going off in 3NT, and those few in 4♡ making just ten tricks.

'That was a smart decision of yours to play in a 4–3 fit rather than bid no-trumps on your lousy club stop, brother!' exclaimed the Little Blue Penguin.

'Well bid and well played', joined in the Jackass, always ready to give credit where credit was due. 'There was nothing we could do, was there, to prevent you from making twelve tricks?'

Just as Archibald was about to reply, the Little Blue Penguin barged in with customary bluntness: 'You shouldn't have put your thought-box on automatic when you made the opening lead', he advised. 'The bidding's told you that I have fewer than fifteen points (since all I could do over 2♣ was make a bid at the two level), with four spades and four or five diamonds. With a 4–4–3–2 shape and 12–14 points I'd have opened 1NT, so I must have five diamonds; I have not rebid them over 2♣, so either they're lousy, or I have longer hearts than clubs, or both. I can't have a club stop, else I'd have bid 2NT over partner's enquiry. Also, you know that I have at most three trumps (since I did not support partner's heart suit immediately). From all this you should be able to guess that I'm likely to have a 4–3–5–1 shape – and the last thing you want is to give old Archie here the opportunity to ruff your winners with my short trumps. A trump lead and a trump continuation when in with a top club', he concluded, 'hold declarer to ten tricks – and should be obvious even to elderly penguins with more fat than bridge sense.'

Awed, the Jackass tried – and failed – to speak. Painfully aware of his own shortcomings, he shot Elspeth an apologetic glance.

'Never mind', she promptly said. 'I wouldn't have found the trump lead either. I bet it's only obvious to penguins who are as lacking in manners as they are in height!'

ARCHIBALD ALLOWED HIMSELF A
BRIEF SMILE AND TABLED HIS HAND

TOO ADVANCED

BY KITTY TELTSCHER

Boris Schapiro, when asked for the best advice he could give bridge players, said laconically: 'Don't play bridge with your wife.' He was perhaps reflecting on the following freak hand which was dealt as a goulash:

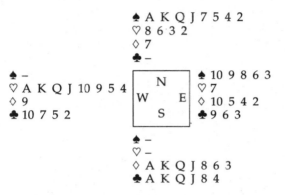

```
                    ♠ A K Q J 7 5 4 2
                    ♡ 8 6 3 2
                    ◇ 7
                    ♣ —

    ♠ —                                 ♠ 10 9 8 6 3
    ♡ A K Q J 10 9 5 4      N           ♡ 7
    ◇ 9                 W       E        ◇ 10 5 4 2
    ♣ 10 7 5 2              S            ♣ 9 6 3

                    ♠ —
                    ♡ —
                    ◇ A K Q J 8 6 3
                    ♣ A K Q J 8 4
```

Boris was sitting North opposite his gorgeous wife Helen. West started the proceedings with 4♡. Boris, sitting non-vulnerable versus vulnerable opponents, overcalled 4♠. The East hand passed.

Helen sat looking at her highly-distributional, powerful hand. Finally, after much thought she made a bid; West passed, and Boris confidently bid 7♠ which – inevitably – was doubled by East.

East led his singleton heart and West cashed four hearts, then played a fifth heart which Boris ruffed high. Now, not even Boris could avoid losing two trump tricks, and the final result was six off doubled! Can you guess what Helen bid? The answer is printed below.

When the dust settled, Boris remarked that the fault was entirely his. Helen's bid had simply been too advanced for him!

Answer: 6♡

FOR WHOM THE BELL TOLLS

BY BARRY RIGAL

The tolling of bells is not usually associated with card games. However, at the bridge table there might be some advantage to having someone ring the bell at critical moments, to warn you of the need to concentrate. The following hand comes from the 1993 *The Sunday Times*/The Macallan Pairs Competition; can you identify the kill point – before it kills you?

♠ A K 5 4 3			
♡ A J 6			
◇ 7 2	N		
♣ 10 8 5	W E		
	S		

	South	West	North	East
♠ 10 8 6 2	1◇	1♠	NB	2♡
♡ K	NB	3♡	NB	4♡
◇ K Q 9 6	End			
♣ A Q 6 4				

You lead the ◇K and partner plays the ◇5 – playing normal methods. Declarer has a reputation for being a slow player, but in fact he wins the first trick in fairly normal tempo and leads the ♡2, which goes to ♡K, ♡A, and ♡3. A small spade from dummy goes to declarer's Queen, partner producing the ♠7. Declarer now plays a second trump to dummy's Jack, partner producing the ♡4, and then – predictably enough – he cashes dummy's top spades to discard the ◇8 and ◇10, partner following high-low. Now declarer plays a club to partner's ♣7 and his ♣K. Can you work out the best defence?

Well, for you to have any chance declarer must have started life with a 1–5–3–4 shape (in fact, this is obvious as soon as declarer produces the ♠Q). You could play partner for the ♣J – but that would simultaneously be playing declarer to have played the clubs in an absurd fashion. Alternatively, of course, you can give partner a club ruff – but that would surely be only three tricks for the defence.

So, it looks as if you need to force declarer: leading a diamond compels him to ruff; he then plays a club, which you win to lead a spade.

Declarer ruffs again and leads a third club, which partner ruffs. Unfortunately, in the two-card ending partner is left with a choice of losing plays: a diamond lead can be ruffed in dummy, a trump leaves declarer with a winning club for trick thirteen.

Paradoxically, things go much better if you lead a spade after winning the first club, as this enables partner to discard his second club. Now you can let him ruff the second club, and play a second diamond. Declarer is forced to ruff again to reach this three-card ending (in which you have, of course, unblocked your diamonds):

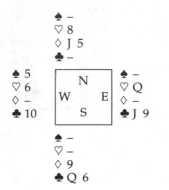

```
            ♠ —
            ♡ 8
            ◇ J 5
            ♣ —
♠ 5                         ♠ —
♡ 6       ┌─────────┐       ♡ Q
◇ —       │    N    │       ◇ —
♣ 10      │ W     E │       ♣ J 9
          │    S    │
          └─────────┘
            ♠ —
            ♡ —
            ◇ 9
            ♣ Q 6
```

With East on lead, declarer cannot take more than one trick.

Well, of course that is only the case if you remembered to retain your fourth club! If you did not, declarer can exit with a club and force you to concede the painful ruff-and-discard.

You don't mean to say that you discarded your *small* club at trick four? Well, never mind, a better player than you did the same.

Perhaps the bell was not ringing loudly enough!

The full deal was:

```
                    ♠ J 9 7
                    ♡ 8 5 4 3
                    ◇ J 5 4 3
                    ♣ 7 2
♠ A K 5 4 3                         ♠ Q
♡ A J 6         ┌─────────┐         ♡ Q 10 9 7 2
◇ 7 2           │    N    │         ◇ A 10 8
♣ 10 8 5        │ W     E │         ♣ K J 9 3
                │    S    │
                └─────────┘
                    ♠ 10 8 6 2
                    ♡ K
                    ◇ K Q 9 6
                    ♣ A Q 6 4
```

This article will also be published in Bridge World magazine.

THE PRINCIPLE OF RESTRICTED CHOICE

BY ANDREW ROBSON

Many players are baffled and confused by the Principle of Restricted Choice (PRC). The reason for this is, probably, that PRC is usually explained in purely mathematical terms. Let's try a different approach.

Imagine that you are playing in 7♠ and that the trump suit (your only worry) is as below:

North
♠ A x x x

South
♠ K 10 x x x

When you cash the Ace, West plays the Jack and when you continue with a low one towards the King, East plays low. Should you play the King, hoping that West started with ♠Q–J doubleton; or should you play the Ten – landing your Grand Slam if West started with a singleton ♠J, but disastrous if he has ♠Q–J?

If the trump suit were as in the diagram below, you would play the Ace and King, correctly remembering the motto *'Eight ever, Nine never'* – meaning that when you are missing the Queen of a suit you should play for the drop when missing four cards, and finesse missing five.

North
♠ A x x x

South
♠ K J x x x

Returning to our original dilemma, it would appear superficially attractive to play the King and 'go for the drop' – after all, we are missing four cards. In fact, it would be wrong. Why? Because of PRC! Consider the two relevant holdings for West: ♠J and ♠Q–J. If he has the Queen-Jack doubleton, *he has a choice*, and therein lies the crux: only half the time will he play the Jack; the other half he will play the Queen.

Thus the fact that he has played the Jack affords the likelihood that he had *no choice* in the matter and that he has the singleton Jack (with a choice, he would be equally likely to play the Queen). Therefore you should finesse, as it is twice as likely that East holds the elusive Queen of trumps!

If you are not convinced, clear your mind and imagine the following (totally non-bridge) scenario…

There is a big sack in which there are two big discs; one has a big letter 'J' on both sides, the other has a big 'J' on one side and a big 'Q' on the other side. You close your eyes and delve into the sack, reaching at random for a disc. You bring it out and lay it flat so that you can only see one side; on opening your eyes you observe that it bears a 'J'. The question is: what's on the other side of the disc? Is it another 'J'? Or a 'Q'?

Let's reason it out. Two of the Js have a 'J' on the other side (each side of the double-faced 'J'), whereas only one has a 'Q' on the other side. The chances are 2:1 that the other side is a 'J'! Although initially you were equally likely to select each of the two discs, the fact that you didn't show a 'Q' means that you have eliminated half the chance of having selected the Q/J disc.

I hope that the analogy is clear. The two-sided 'J' disc represents the holding of the singleton Jack; the 'Q–J' disc represents Q–J doubleton. Back to the Grand Slam: the fact that West played specifically the Jack halves the chances of him hiding Q–J doubleton.

Had West played specifically the Queen, the same argument would apply: it would be almost twice as likely to be singleton as part of Q–J doubleton. Thus whichever honour West plays, it is likely to be singleton. An expert will always go down in this Grand Slam if West has Q–J doubleton!

Now let's consider a few more holdings and examine the implications of PRC.

North

♠ A J 10

South

♠ x x x

You play low to the Ten; it loses to the King. On regaining the lead, you have to decide whether to take a second finesse in this suit. In other words, is the Queen of this suit equally likely to be in each of the opponents' hands?

Answer: it is twice as likely to be with West (in the opposite hand to the King). Remember: the fact that East played the King affords the presumption that he did not have a choice, or he might have played the Queen.

North
♠ A Q 10
South
♠ x x x

You play low to the Ten; it loses to the Jack. Is your second finesse, that against the King, a better than even-money proposition? Is this a PRC situation?

Answer: no! The position of the King is exactly 50/50. Why? Because if East has the King and the Jack, he has no choice this time: when you finesse the Ten, he will *always* play the Jack, never the King.

Does PRC apply in the following positions, and why?

Diagram 1
North
Q J x
South
x x x

You lead low to the Jack (or Queen), losing to the King. Is the location of the Ace 50/50, or is one opponent more likely to hold it than the other?

Diagram 2
North
A x x x
South
K J 9 x x

You cash the Ace on which West plays the Ten; you lead a low card towards the K–J–9 and East follows low. Do you finesse the Jack or play the King?

Diagram 3
North
A x x
South
K Q 9 x

When you cash the King and the Ace, West follows with a low card,

34

then the Ten. You lead a third round from North and East follows low. Where is the Jack?

In the position outlined in **Diagram 1**, PRC applies: the fact that the Jack lost specifically to East's *King* affords the presumption that he had no choice – thus West is twice as likely to hold the Ace.

Diagram 2 is a different kettle of fish: no player holding Q–10 doubleton would be silly enough to play the Queen under the Ace. The fact that the Ten was played does not alter the original odds: '*Eight ever, Nine never*'. You should play the King on the second round as normal.

In the situation illustrated in **Diagram 3**, however, you must finesse! West played the Ten as opposed to the Jack. If he had a choice, he would have played the Jack half the time. He did not. It is twice as likely that he *could* not play the Jack (he did not have it) than that he *chose* not to play the Jack. If you knew West, and knew that he would always play the Ten before the Jack, then PRC would not apply – you would play the Queen on the third round. But no one knows the foibles of the opponents.

Make sure you can recognize PRC positions – they occur when two cards of equal rank could be played (e.g. the Queen or King, the 9 or the Ten, the Ten or the Queen after the Jack has been played, etc.). When one opponent plays one of these cards, the other opponent is almost twice as likely to hold the other one. Even if you don't quite understand *why* PRC works, make sure that you can recognize it and use it. You will start to 'guess' correctly much more often, and the uninitiated will start to hold their cards closer to their chests!

This article is reprinted by kind permission of BRIDGE PLUS.

THE PLAYERS WERE TALKING ALL THE TIME

Before the finals of the Open Team at the 11th Asian Bridge Club Championships, the recorders (female students of the University of Trisakti) were coached how to record the bidding and the play. They were told that since the bidding was done with bidding boxes, the players did not talk to each other. After the first match, the recorders came back to their Chief, and excitedly told him that the players were talking all the time. The Chief asked what the players were saying.

'Small club please', was the reply.

(from the IBPA Bulletin)

BRIDGE IN BRITAIN IS 100 YEARS OLD

BY SIMON AINGER

O ne evening in 1894, Lord Brougham and Vaux, a descendant of the first Baron who designed the famous carriage, settled down to play a game of Whist at the Portland Club. As dealer, he should have exposed the final card to determine the trump suit: instead, he placed it face-down on his own stack, forgetting that he was not playing Bridge – a game that was very popular in the South of France, from where he had just returned. His explanation aroused great interest and a determination amongst the members to try out the new game.

So popular did it become that, within the year, the Portland Club set up a committee, liaising with a similar body from the Turf Club, to establish and publish *The Laws of Bridge*. The year 1994 therefore marks the centenary of the start of Bridge in Britain.

The game at that time had a very different format from that which we know today, but the modern player would find much that is familiar. Bridge is, of course, a derivative of Whist, but the vital variations introduced (the exposure of one hand as 'dummy', the fact that the dealer or his partner could determine the trump suit or elect to have 'no trumps', and new scoring) made it a much greater challenge and ensured its popularity.

The next major development of the game came within almost a decade with the arrival of Auction Bridge and, as the name implies, the introduction of bidding to determine the trump suit and thereby who played the hand. The first *Laws of Auction Bridge* were published in 1908.

At about the same time a game called 'Plafond', with many similarities to Bridge, was becoming popular in France, and the next revolution came via America in the 1920s when H.S. Vanderbilt applied the Plafond system of scoring to Bridge.

Essentially, the change meant that only tricks 'contracted' to be made counted towards the score for game. Previously all tricks made could be scored below the line. This seemingly small change had a dramatic effect, and led to the birth of Contract Bridge – basically the game we know today.

Reprinted from The 1994 Collins Bridge Diary by kind permission of the publishers.

A GOOD LEAD

Rowlands: 'That would have been a good lead, partner!'

Selway: 'Last time I found a good lead there was an Alsatian at the end of it!'

David Barnes

TOO LATE

BY TONY PARKINSON

The top division of the Berks & Bucks CBA Teams-of-four League tends to be a very close affair. The competing teams are uncommonly well-matched and it is not unusual, at the end of the season, to find that you might be playing for the championship and to avoid relegation in the same match.

Our first match this year was as even as usual. There were, though, several hands where intellectual effort might have been worthwhile and well rewarded. The hand featured was the second board of the match at my table. Consider the problem first from my point of view. I was the non-vulnerable West in 3NT with the following in sight:

♠ K 10 6 3
♡ A K Q 3
◇ A 8
♣ A 9 4

N
W   E
S

♠ 7 5 2
♡ 8 6 2
◇ Q 9 4 3
♣ K 7 5

The bidding was brief: Pass from East and South, 2NT from me, Pass from North, and 3NT from East. North led the ♣Q.

It all looks depressingly familiar. To make, this contract needs the hearts to break 3–3, the ◇K and ♠A to be right, and the minor suits distributed so that the defence cannot cash too many when they finally get going. And – as my old granny used to say – 'Pigs might fly.'

Still, it's always right to duck the opening lead, so North continues with the ♣J. Since I need the ♣K as the entry to the ◇Q once that is set up, I win this trick in hand, then cash the ♡A–K. Things now begin to look up, since both defenders appear to have an odd number of hearts and indeed both follow to the ♡Q. Knowing a good thing when I see one, I cash the fourth heart. North goes into a coma, from which he eventually emerges with the ♠J, while South ditches a club, having now played increasingly smaller clubs on each occasion. Next I play the ◇A, followed by a second diamond on which North plays the ◇J, the ◇Q holding the trick. What next?

We know that North started with three hearts, presumably four clubs, and at least three diamonds to the King. If his distribution is 3–3–3–4, it appears that he has the ♠A, ◇K, and one club left. The winning line then is to cash the ♣K, exit with a diamond, and let North give you a spade after he has cashed his winners. However, North could equally well have started with a 2–3–4–4 shape, with four diamonds (presumably to the K–J–10), and either ♠A–J or ♠Q–J. In this case, the winning line is to play on the spades first, and make sure you get it right. I think that the line you might eliminate, on a sort of Restricted-Choice argument, is for North to have the ♠Q–J, since he might equally have played the ♠Q originally. So you toss up mentally – and get it wrong.

North did have the 3–3–3–4 shape and, by not taking the ◊K when he was given the opportunity, he has given you the chance to make this contract had you read the situation correctly – as South was quick to point out to North. In fact, by discarding the ♠J, North has given you the contract, since you can now just duck two spades and he cannot get to his diamond trick. What he must do is to discard a diamond on the fourth heart. Then you cannot prevent him from coming to two spades, two clubs and a diamond.

It would appear, then, that you are stuck, and that the defence are always going to prevail. Well, curiously, no – that is not the case. If you don't duck the opening club lead, then you will have a spare card with which to throw North in at the appropriate moment, so he will have no recourse but to give you a spade trick.

MESSAGE FROM ON HIGH

At the end of the EBU's National Women's Teams Congress, one of the directors was heard to say: 'Will the late occupant of Room 235 please approach the control table.'

(from the Berks & Bucks CBA Bulletin)

MURDER AT THE TABLE

BY MARTIN HOFFMAN

T he Bridge Pairs Marathon played over twenty-four hours at the Young Chelsea Bridge Club is one of the most prestigious events staged in London.

With only short intervals for tea and coffee breaks, sometimes three players join forces and compete as one pair – which gives each person a chance to have a rest. In 1965 I was one of a two-man partnership, the other player being Zia Mahmood. On that occasion a terrible tragedy took place.

At 5.00 in the morning, during the third tea-break, I saw the proprietor, Warwick Pitch, come into the bridge room ashen-faced, announcing that a body had been found dead on the third floor – assumed murdered. The victim was Al Rose, a Romanian gypsy and a bridge professional. Warwick immediately called in the police, who brought in Scotland Yard's Chief Inspector Claude Simpson of Homicide to take charge. Inspector Simpson was not only a leading detective, but also the Yard's top bridge expert. There were four primary suspects: myself and Zia, Boris Nicholevitch, and Atta Gengis Khan.

Boris and Atta had been competing as a threesome together with Al Rose, so naturally they were the prime suspects. I had the perfect alibi, as Zia had put me in a difficult small slam, and I was still trying to figure out how to make it when the body was discovered. Zia too had a perfect alibi, as he had spent the interval in the bar with two beautiful blondes.

Inspector Simpson tried to discover the backgrounds of each suspect. He knew that I was a Czech refugee who made a living backing winners on the horses. Zia was an accountant, who was also involved in developing real estate for wealthy Arabs from the Gulf. Atta was a direct descendant of the great conqueror Gengis Khan – a notorious overbidder, who after three centuries had still not learned that over-aggression does not pay. Boris also came from famous stock, being a direct descendant of Czar Nicholas, better known as Ivan the Terrible. He is reputed to have spent fifty years in the Siberian Salt Mines, where apparently he was responsible for the deaths of thousands of bridge players. These prisoners were so weakened by lack of food and con-

40

stant torture by the KGB, that one look of disapproval from Boris was enough to cause a heart attack – proving the old cliché that 'looks can kill'. He came to England in his early sixties, when an Arabian Prince – moved by his story – paid a king's ransom to have him released.

These were the two deals relevant to the case which Inspector Simpson studied:

Dealer: South
N/S Vul

♠ A 8 3
♡ K 7 6 2
◊ A 5 3
♣ K 9 2

♠ 9 6		♠ 5 4 2
♡ 4	N	♡ A 10 9 8 5
◊ Q J 9 7 6	W E	◊ 10 4
♣ Q J 10 8 7	S	♣ 6 5 4

♠ K Q J 10 7
♡ Q J 3
◊ K 8 2
♣ A 3

South	West	North	East
Zia	Boris	Me	Al
1♠	2NT	Dbl	3♣
NB	NB	4♣	NB
6NT	End		

Zia won the opening lead of the ♣Q with his Ace, and played the ♡3 to the King. Al won with the Ace and returned a club. All Zia had to do now was cash his winners and squeeze Boris in diamonds and clubs. Boris was not very pleased; he explained to Al that it was important to duck the ♡K – and to duck the second round of clubs also. This way there would have been no pressure, and the contract would have failed.

This was the second deal:

Dealer: North
Game All

♠ A Q 7 2
♡ A 2
◊ A K Q 3
♣ 4 3 2

♠ 10		♠ K J 6 4
♡ 10 9 8 5 4	N	♡ Q J 3
◊ 10 8 7 6	W E	◊ J 9 4
♣ 10 8 7	S	♣ Q J 5

♠ 9 8 5 3
♡ K 7 6
◊ 5 2
♣ A K 9 6

South	West	North	East
Zia	Boris	Me	Al
		1◊	NB
1♠	NB	2♣	NB
3♣	NB	5♠	End

West led the ♡10. Zia won with the Ace in dummy and played a small club to his King, everybody following small. He continued with the ♠3 to the ♠10, dummy's ♠Q, and the ♠K from East. Al returned the ♣Q, Zia won and cashed the ♡K; then he ruffed a heart with the ♠2 and continued with the ◊A–K–Q, discarding a club. This was the position when he now played the fourth diamond from dummy:

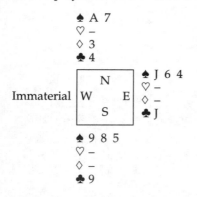

```
            ♠ A 7
            ♡ –
            ◊ 3
            ♣ 4
                        ♠ J 6 4
               N        ♡ –
Immaterial  W     E     ◊ –
               S        ♣ J
            ♠ 9 8 5
            ♡ –
            ◊ –
            ♣ 9
```

When the ◊3 was played from dummy, East was in big trouble. If he ruffed small, declarer would overruff and throw him in with a club. If he ruffed with the ♠J, declarer would just discard his last club – and if he discarded a club, declarer would ruff and play his losing club forcing East to ruff and lead away from his ♠J–6.

Boris was furious. He explained to Al that when the first club was played from the dummy, he should have played a high club – and that when the second club was played he should have completed the unblock by following with his second honour. The ending would now have been completely different: when the fourth diamond is played, East has to ruff small and declarer can overruff – but is left with two more losers.

Atta Gengis Khan had a cast-iron alibi, as he had spent the break surrounded by five admiring females. He seemed more popular than Elvis Presley! Boris, on the other hand, could remember nothing that had happened during the interval.

The case was never solved, as there was insufficient evidence for the prosecution. However, Inspector Simpson has his suspicions as to who was the guilty party!

TONY'S PLAY PROBLEM

BY TONY FORRESTER

You are South, declarer in 6♡.

West leads the ◊K, which you ruff. On the ♡A, East shows out.

How do you continue?

Solution on page 211.

♠ A K 3 2
♡ 4 3 2
◊ Q 5
♣ A K J 10

♠ 7 6
♡ A K Q J 10 9
◊ –
♣ 9 8 7 6 5

This article is reprinted by kind permission of BRIDGE PLUS.

BULLETS AND MINIS

As is the case in many activities, bridge too has its jargon. If words like 'bullets' and 'minis' evoke images of players shooting it out to settle the post-mortem and of long, scantily clad legs, you may find conversation difficult at some bridge tables. And what about the expression 'Green vs Red'? Nothing to do with traffic-lights, but with being Non-Vulnerable vs Vulnerable opponents. Now you will not find it surprising that 'Bullets' are Aces, and the 'Mini' is a Mini No-trump (i.e. a balanced hand with 10–12 points).

Sometimes lack of familiarity with bridge terms may lead to embarrassing situations. A novice friend of mine was refused entry at a 'Flitch'; his deep mortification at not being deemed worthy turned into relieved laughter when he was told that this type of event is open only to married couples. His chances of success – playing with a male partner – would have been somewhat slim!

A CAUSERIE ON BRIDGE

BY PAT COTTER

Only the other day, in May 1993, this hand occurred. Please study the Big Question:

```
              ♠ A K 10 9 3
              ♡ K 7 6 4 2
              ◇ K 7 4
              ♣ —
♠ J 8 7 4      ┌─────────┐      ♠ Q 6 2
♡ Q 10         │    N    │      ♡ A
◇ J 10 2       │ W     E │      ◇ A 8 3
♣ 10 6 3 2     │    S    │      ♣ K 9 8 7 5 4
               └─────────┘
              ♠ 5
              ♡ J 9 8 5 3
              ◇ Q 9 6 5
              ♣ A Q J
```

I was playing *partie fixe* with quite a good player, but an undisciplined bidder. Sitting North, I dealt at a Love score, and opened the bidding with 1♠. East overcalled with 2♣, and my partner said 2♡. West came in with 3♣, I jumped to 4♡, East went on to 5♣, and my partner said 5♡.

After this confident bid by South I thought that there must be a chance of making a slam, so I said 6♡ – prepared to apologise if the slam turned out to be unmakeable.

West led the ♣2, and I felt the first twinge of anxiety when my partner discarded a spade from the table. East played the King, which lost to the Ace. South then led a low heart towards dummy. West produced the ♡10, and my King was taken by the Ace. The ◇A was cashed, and with West having to score the trump Queen, the result was two down.

The cards were tabled. Suddenly I caught sight of South's ♣Q–J and, although I am not given to criticizing partners, I could not help asking, 'Why didn't you double 5♣?'

Ignoring my question, South turned to East and asked, 'Was your ♡A singleton?' On receiving an affirmative reply South, with a meaningful look at me, said, 'If I had played for that, I should have made my 5♡ contract.'

The problem was solved. It was all my fault for making that idiotic bid of 6♡. Somehow I refrained from saying, 'If you had discarded my three diamonds on your ♣A–Q–J, and then played for the singleton ♡A in East's hand, you would have brought home the slam.'

The Big Question is: 'Is there anyone else in the world who would not have doubled 5♣?'

ROLL OVER, HOUDINI!

BY ZIA MAHMOOD

It's rare that bridge players receive compliments – but when they do come, the one that strokes my ego the most is the word 'magician'. You can keep your praises for error-free bridge, or the accolades given to the so-called purity of computer-like relay bids – they don't do anything for me. No, I suppose it's something in my character that has always made me thrilled by the razzle-dazzle of the spectacular, and excited by the flamboyant and the extraordinary. Yet, the world of bridge magic, like stage magic, is often no more than an illusion, much simpler to perform than it appears to the watcher. Allow me to take you into that world.

Assume you are East, sitting over the dummy, North, after the bidding has gone 1NT by South on your left, 3NT on your right. Isolating one suit (let's say diamonds), you see that dummy has:

either	J 2	while you have	Q 4
or	J 3 2	or	Q 5 4
		or	Q 6 5 4

Declarer plays the Jack from dummy. What would you do? Cover, you say? Correct. With Q–4 and Q–5–4 you would cover all the time. With Q–6–5–4 you would cover somewhere between usually and always.

Good! What if the bidding was 1♡ on your left, 4♡ on your right, and dummy had in a side suit:

either	Q 2	while you had	K 4
or	Q 3 2	or	K 5 4
		or	K 6 5 4

Declarer played the Queen from dummy. Again, what would you do? Again, the answer is easy. With K–4 and K–5–4 you would cover all the time. With K–6–5–4 you would cover somewhere between usually and always.

In both examples, you would have defended correctly, following one of bridge's oldest rules, *'Cover an honour with an honour'*. Bear with me a moment longer and change seats – taking the place of the declarer who needs as many tricks as possible (don't we always?). How would you play these suits?

Run the Jack, run the Queen? That's normal; you would be following the simple, basic rule taught to every beginner about the finesse. But hold it a moment. Something's wrong. How can both these plays be right? If in the first example we saw that the defender over the dummy

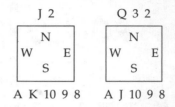

J 2

Q 3 2

A K 10 9 8   A J 10 9 8

would nearly always (correctly) cover the honour played, when he had it, how can it be right to finesse that honour when we know that East (RHO) almost never has it? The Queen in the first example, and the King in the second, are almost surely in the West hand (*mal placé*, as the French say) and *sometimes unprotected*. My Bols Tip, therefore (and I certainly have taken my time to get there), is as simple and easy as this: *When they don't cover, they don't have it*, and declarer should place or drop the relevant card offside – even when this is hugely anti-percentage. Before the critics jump, I must add a few provisos:

1. The length must be in the concealed hand.
2. The declarer should not be known to have special length or strength in the suit.
3. The honours in dummy should not be touching, i.e. J–10, Q–J, etc.
4. The pips in the suit should be solid enough to afford overtaking your honour without costing a trick when the suit breaks badly.

I know this tip is going to revolutionize the simple fundamentals of the everyday finesse, but although it comes with no guarantees, I can assure you that it is nearly always effective and *deadly*. Here are two examples – both from actual play:

Deal 1

♠ K Q 3 2
♡ A 4 3
♦ J 2
♣ K J 6 5

```
       N
   W       E
       S
```

♠ A 4
♡ 6 5 2
♦ A K 10 9 5
♣ 10 7

Deal 2

♠ Q 2
♡ 5 3
♦ 10 9 4
♣ A K 10 9 7 2

```
       N
   W       E
       S
```

♠ A J 10
♡ K 2
♦ A K Q 3
♣ Q 6 5 3

46

Deal 1. You reach 3NT after opening a slightly off-beat weak 1NT (if you weren't off-beat, you wouldn't still be reading this), West leads a heart, and you win the third heart with the Ace and lead the ◊ J. East plays low – he didn't cover! He doesn't have it! Drop the Queen off-side! Magic – you might have thought so, before you read this article.
Deal 2. Finally, you reach 6♣ from the right side (well bid) and receive a trump lead. How would you play?

The scientists would carefully look at this hand and see that the percentage line would be to draw trumps and play ◊A–K–Q – if the diamonds were 3–3, or the Jack came down, they would discard a heart from the dummy. Now they could play up to the ♡K and, if that lost, they would finally try the finesse in spade. Not bad, you say? True, but the greatest illusionist of all times, Harry Houdini, would have rejected this line. Instead, he would have played the ♠Q at trick two. No East living in the twentieth century would fail to cover with the King if he had it (declarer might have A–J–3, for example). If East played low, Houdini would *know* that the King was in the West hand and win with the Ace. He would now draw trumps and play on diamonds. If they weren't good, he too would play a heart up, but if they were good, he would discard a spade, not a heart, from dummy, and take a ruffing finesse against West's ♠K, setting up the ♠10 for a heart discard to make his contract with both finesses wrong.

If at that time the kibitzers burst into applause and the deep-throated voice of Ella Fitzgerald, singing that 'Old Black Magic', could be heard in the distance, don't be surprised. Roll over, Houdini, the bridge magicians are coming!

Zia Mahmood won the prestigious Bols Tips competition in 1990 with the article printed above.

THE IMPORTANCE OF BEING EARNEST

The club expert was showing off. On receiving the lead of ♠K against his 3NT contract, he enquired of the novice on his right whether she and her partner played 'Roman' leads.

RHO was perplexed but helpful. 'I don't know what foreigners do', she said, 'but I have the Ace, so if *you* don't have it partner must have the Queen!'

CROSSWORD PUZZLE

BY DON PUTNAM

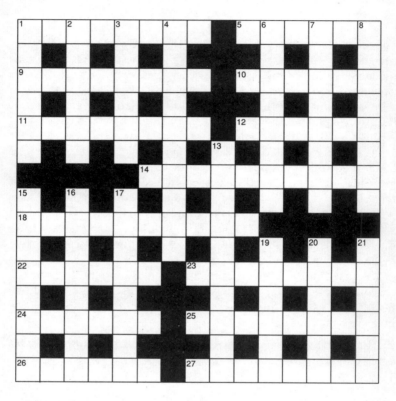

ACROSS:

1 Note the insignficance of giving me a Queen and two little spades. (8)

5 A cue-bid would have…catered for holding a whale. (6)

9 The Culbertsons swallowing lettuce with merriment. (8)

10 A patience game is for fanatics. (6)

11 Setbacks, high and low? (8)

12 Has to break up post-mortem with one type of walking stick perhaps. (6)

14 Star-gazer uses convention against North when getting his measure. (10)

18 What the pompously-mouthed bridge player shows, spattering you with – not dirt! (10)

22 Note the high-low, says this parrot. (2-4)

23 Small capitals will be placed before a lot of common people in this board game. (8)

24 Malay dagger caught by pre-eminent bridge author. (6)

25 He has superb technical skill – using the six before the king – turning out thus. (8)

26 Dog that compiles crosswords. (6)

27 Inspector-General breaks in honestly, exposing 'unhallowed flirtation between Queen and Knave'. (8)

DOWN:

1 Married woman holds Ace, Jack, nothing, in two suits. (6)

2 Look at a fellow holding left bower. (6)

3 Inquisitive persons could be sore after North–South had dropped off. (6)

4 That which The Gold Cup is not, needing addition of team for one's table perhaps. (10)

6 Dummy that can be entered by amateur or professional worker. (4, 4)

7 Micros simply search for a method of bridge scoring. (5-3)

8 Desmond goes to bridge event and loses hope. (8)

13 Rice pot not cooked for use of competitive bidders. (10)

15 Twelve of their own HCPs for Jacoby, Burnstine, Schenken and Gottlieb. (4, 4)

16 Howell perhaps shows what wood-pushers do on time. (8)

17 Is it right to swallow bridge rival's potatoes? (8)

19 Bridge player of some competence is right to support Mixed Teams. (6)

20 Not being square, old boy is attracted to a type of whist. (6)

21 Opener's last raise is a violation of the rules. (6)

Solution on page 212.

With thanks to Tom Simm, who solved this puzzle in one hour!

AT SIXES AND SEVENS

BY BOB ROWLANDS

The first session of the recent Tollemache Qualifying Round, the English Bridge Union's competition for County teams-of-eight, was as usual a chastening experience. Eighth equal out of nine teams-of-eight in our group, the in-between-session post-mortem was somewhat painful. Board 13 seemed innocent enough with the same bidding and opening lead at all four tables – yet we still managed four minus scores:

Dealer: South
Game All

```
                              ♠ 6 4
                              ♡ K Q 10 8 5 2
                              ◊ J 10 8
                              ♣ A 2
        ♠ A 7 3          ┌─────────┐      ♠ 5
        ♡ 4 3            │    N    │      ♡ A J 9
        ◊ K Q 9 5 2    W │         │ E    ◊ A 7 6 3
        ♣ K 7 5          │    S    │      ♣ J 10 9 8 4
                         └─────────┘
```

South	West	North	East	
3♠	End			♠ K Q J 10 9 8 2
				♡ 7 6
				◊ 4
				♣ Q 6 3

We were North–South at Tables One and Three, and East–West at Tables Two and Four.

At Table One, the opponents' West led the ◊K and switched to the ♠3. Declarer won in hand and led the ♡6 to ♡4, ♡K, and ♡A, then East returned the ♣J to ♣Q, ♣K, and ♣2. West now cashed the ♠A and returned the ♣5, won by dummy's Ace. Declarer did his best by ruffing a diamond and running all his trumps, but East won the last trick with the ♡J for one down, and 100 to East–West.

The play at Table Two took an identical course, except that after cashing the ♠A, our West returned the ♣7 instead of ♣5. With West now unable to beat declarer's ♣6, East was squeezed in clubs and hearts, and North–South scored plus 140.

At Table Three the opponents' West continued diamonds, declarer ruffed and led a heart to dummy's King, but East carefully ducked.

Declarer continued hearts, so East won and returned the ♠5 to ♠K, ♠A, and ♠4. West carefully continued with the ♠7, leaving declarer with no answer – 100 to East–West.

At Table Four everything was the same up to the trump lead. Our West won the first spade and returned... the ♠3. Declarer gratefully won in dummy with the ♠6, ruffed out East's ♡A, drew the last trump, and with the ♣A still in dummy made an overtrick – plus 170 to North–South!

Notice that if West continues diamonds at trick two and East wins the first heart lead, declarer always prevails even if East makes the best return of the ♣J. Declarer simply ducks the first club, leaving West powerless. At the tables where West switched to the ♠3 at trick two, perhaps declarer should have won the ♣A and returned a club. East must play low, and let West win the ♣7 to continue trumps – not easy!

As one of our team ruefully remarked after surveying the damage caused by our misuse of the ♠7 and ♠6, as well as ♣7 and ♣6, 'No doubt about it: we were all at sixes and sevens!'

The IMP scores with our North–South pairs both minus 100, and our East–West pairs respectively minus 140 and minus 170? We lost six, six, seven, and seven IMPs!

QU'EST-CE THE LAST BID?

At the first European Mixed Championships held in Bordeaux in 1990, bidding boxes and screens greatly contributed to making the bridge a most serious affair.

However, they were no proof against Gallic wit: after three passes, our French opponent held up a 'Pass' card shown only to his lady opponent on his side of the screen, then put down a card displaying '7NT' and passed this through to us. His wife dutifully entered this on her score card when her husband stood up to laugh and share the joke with all of us.

Brian Overy

DECISION TIME

BY MIKE WHITTAKER

As a defender, a holding of A–Q–x in the trump suit is quite nice, if not all that common. It is even nicer when the opponents bid to a small slam – but it does not look quite so good when the trump suit is as follows:

Dummy
K J 10 x x

Declarer
x x x x

When South leads a small trump, West might hesitate for a split second – and that should be all the help that South needs. A better West will have thought about it beforehand and might resort to a bit of deception, rising with the Ace and continuing with the small trump. This is well known, but can still succeed against an inexperienced South. Is there anything else West might do in this situation to cause South to go wrong?

In certain circumstances, I think there is. Take a look at this hand from the recent semi-final of a county pairs event:

Dealer: East
N/S Vul.

♠ A K J 10 6 2
♡ K J 10 6 3
◇ A Q
♣ –

♠ 9 5
♡ A Q 7
◇ 9 7 6 5 3 2
♣ 4 2

N
W　E
S

♠ 8 3
♡ 5
◇ J 10 4
♣ A Q J 9 8 7 3

♠ Q 7 4
♡ 9 8 4 2
◇ K 8
♣ K 10 6 5

After East opened with 3♣, South became the declarer in 6♡ after North had shown a very powerful two-suiter. West led the ♣4, which South ruffed in dummy. After overtaking the ◇Q with the ◇K, South led the ♡9 and it was soon all over, with West's promising trump holding taking just one trick.

Even if West had gone up with the ♡A and continued clubs, forcing South to ruff in dummy, South could still have returned to hand with a spade for a finesse against the ♡Q.

A while later I realized that West had missed a chance to make life very difficult for South. In view of North's known powerful two-suited hand, West was quite likely to be in the position shown at the start of this article. Anticipating this, West might have *led* the ♡A and continued with the ♡7. Would you have finessed at trick two?

THE GUTHRIE FIVE

BY NIGEL GUTHRIE

You will have heard of the 'Whitfield Six' – the father of all end-game problems. Below is a new type of end-game quiz, a double-dummy speed test that has defeated several experts.

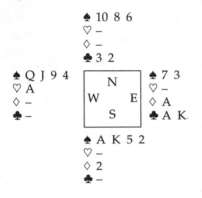

Can you find more than one solution within *five* minutes?

Spades are trumps. West is on lead. South is to make four out of five tricks.

Solution on page 212.

UNNATURAL PLAY

BY P F SAUNDERS

I claimed my contract, and with it the rubber, and glanced at my two young opponents. They were already entering the score, and seemed to have no comment to make on the final hand of the evening. My partner, Paddy, was examining the cards of the last few unplayed tricks that had been ceded. I caught his eye, and knew that he was thinking what I was thinking.

It turned out that my granddaughter and her partner, Bruce, were just up on us at the end, and we congratulated them on their improved defence. 'Only on the very last hand', Paddy told her, 'did you allow your aged relative to get away with it.'

'I couldn't make out what he was up to.'

Dealer: West
Game All

	♠ J 5 3
	♡ 10 8 6 5
	◊ 10 7 3
	♣ A K 8

♠ K 10 9 6 2
♡ A 7 3
◊ 2
♣ Q 10 6 5

```
      N
  W       E
      S
```

♠ A 8 7 4
♡ 4
◊ K Q 8 4
♣ J 4 3 2

South	West	North	East
	NB	NB	NB
1♡	1♠	2♡	3♠
4♡	End		

♠ Q
♡ K Q J 9 2
◊ A J 9 6 5
♣ 9 7

'He saw – and so, I expect, did you – that West's opening lead, the ◊2, was likely to be a singleton. It ran to your Queen and his Ace, and now he crossed to dummy's ♣K, and continued with the ♣A. As soon as he did that, you should have asked yourself what he had in mind (he had not crossed in order to lead trumps), and when he went on to lead the ♣8, you could have found an answer.'

'I found one all right when he discarded the ♠Q instead of ruffing. He was at his favourite business of exchanging one loser for another.

He does it just to confuse me!'

'Look at it from my point of view', I broke in. 'I could see three certain losers, and that opening lead suggested the danger of a fourth loser – a diamond ruff by West. I had to try to keep you, East, out of the lead, which you might win at any moment with one of two Aces. If you held the ♡A, I was done for. If you held the ♠A, I might be able to prevent your using it by discarding my singleton spade. I'd lose a club trick that way, but prevent a diamond ruff.'

'I see now. It was one of those Scissors Coups, wasn't it? And it came off because I had the wrong Ace. Lucky old you.'

'I don't understand', put in her partner, Bruce, who is the slower of the two, but often the more practical. 'According to Paddy we ought to have stopped you. I had to win that third club lead, and couldn't find anything better to do than lead out Ace and another heart, after which the declarer drew the last trump, conceded a diamond, and claimed the rest. I suppose he must have won four trumps, four diamonds, and two clubs.'

'You ought not to have had to win the third club', said Paddy.

There was a moment's silence, broken by an agonised, 'Oh, no!' from my granddaughter, as the light broke. 'At last I'm there', she lamented. 'I ought to have gone up with my Jack on the third round of clubs instead of automatically following with the ♣4.'

'Yes', said Paddy. 'Admittedly, Bruce could have played his ♣Q–10 under the ♣A–K, but that's a lot to ask – and it could be quite dangerous. If you rise with the ♣J, declarer would have had to ruff, or let you have the lead, and he'd have gone down.'

'I do apologize, Bruce. What I still can't understand is how such an artful, devious grandfather managed to acquire such a natural, straightforward granddaughter!'

ETHICS CORNER

In the game of life, it is better to score by honours than by tricks.

Olive Crisp

MAKING LIFE DIFFICULT

BY ANDREW KAMBITES

We all have our pet bridge hate. Mine is the self-satisfied post-mortem expert who regards failure to explore every nook and cranny to seek out a slam as a heinous crime. As he indulges his quest for perfection, he accepts his all-too-frequently unsuccessful sorties to the five level as the inevitable consequence of expert martyrdom.

For example, I remember being the object of criticism for jumping to 4♠ at unfavourable vulnerability over an opposing 3♣ pre-empt with:

♠ A Q J 10 5 3 2	A slam was missed when	♠ K 6 4
♡ K Q 6	partner turned up with:	♡ J 10 9
◊ A Q 4		◊ 7 5 2
♣ –		♣ A K 5 2

Yes, a far from ideal result, but worth 9 IMPs when my counterpart at the other table made an 'expert' double (regarding his hand as too strong for 4♠). This was passed out, and 3♣ went just two off!

Now, give your opening bids with the hands below, first in hand, vulnerable *vs* non-vulnerable.

Hand 1	**Hand 2**
♠ A 6 5	♠ K Q J 9 6 3
♡ A	♡ J 7
◊ –	◊ A Q 4 3 2
♣ A 10 9 8 7 6 5 4 3	♣ –

With **Hand 1** I opened 5♣. Do you regard it as a crime to pre-empt with three Aces? Consider the complete layout at the top of page 57.

Do you blame East for protecting with 5◊? It cost him minus 800!

At the other table, South bided time with 1♣. West's 1♡ overcall brought forth a negative double from North (showing four spades). East jumped to 5◊, and what is South now supposed to do? He has shown four clubs, but he has nine! A 6♣ bid brought forth a sharp double, and the inevitable one down. Plus 14 IMPs.

Hand 1

Dealer: South
N/S Vul

```
                    ♠ K J 7 2
                    ♡ 8 7 3 2
                    ◊ Q 10 9 7 4
                    ♣ –
♠ Q 8 4 3                           ♠ 10 9
♡ K J 10 9 6 4      N               ♡ Q 5
◊ –             W       E           ◊ A K J 8 6 5 3 2
♣ K Q 2             S               ♣ J
                    ♠ A 6 5
                    ♡ A
                    ◊ –
                    ♣ A 10 9 8 7 6 5 4 3
```

It was my partner's chance to shine, holding **Hand 2**. He opened 4♠!
Yes, I know that 6◊ could be lay-down, but again judge the bid by its
results.

Hand 2

Dealer: North
N/S Vul

```
                    ♠ K Q J 9 6 3
                    ♡ J 7
                    ◊ A Q 4 3 2
                    ♣ –
♠ 7 5                               ♠ A 4
♡ A 10 9 5 3        N               ♡ K 8 4 2
◊ 8 7           W       E           ◊ J
♣ A 10 9 8          S               ♣ K Q 7 6 5 2
                    ♠ 10 8 2
                    ♡ Q 6
                    ◊ K 10 9 6 5
                    ♣ J 4 3
```

Actually 4♠ can be beaten – courtesy of a diamond ruff — but it made.
Plus 620.

At the other table North opened 1♠, giving East–West an easy entry
into the auction. A 5♣ contract by West, doubled and made with an
overtrick, was worth plus 650. This time plus 15 IMPs.

These three hands brought in 38 IMPs, and in each case the theme
was the same.

Forget about pie-in-the-sky slams. Concentrate on making life simple for yourself and difficult for your opponents.

Sadly, I must resign myself to the knowledge that one missed slam
after an 'unsound' pre-empt will again bring the scientific vultures out
in force!

A HANDSOME COUP

BY JANE BODIN

The handsome stranger arrived just before the start of the week's duplicate. Happily I offered myself as his partner – after all, being in charge does entitle one to some perks. Wolverhampton Bridge Club is not a candidate for a Mills & Boon location, but there is always hope, and our visitor could have graced any front cover.

THE HANDSOME STRANGER ARRIVED JUST BEFORE THE START OF THE WEEK'S DUPLICATE

With little time to write out a convention card, we agreed to play Benjaminised Acol, with the opening 2NT to show 19–20 points. We touched briefly on Stayman and Transfers – then off we went into the night.

Fortune favoured us in the early rounds, but alas the course of true partnership understanding rarely runs smooth.

Third in hand as West I picked up an interesting hand with a seven-card club suit:

♠ –
♡ A 10 6
♢ 7 5 3
♣ A J 9 8 7 6 4

My partner opened 2NT. Oh, if we had only had more time at the start of the evening to discuss our system! Dreams of 6NT or 7♣, nightmares of 3NT not even making, were all possibilities. But tonight was the night for adventure. Throwing decorum and discretion to the winds, I gazed into his burning eyes and bid 6♣. Would I have made that leap in the dark with another? Who can tell!

The ◇ A was led, and dummy faced:

```
♠ –                          ♠ A K J 2
♡ A 10 6         N           ♡ K 9 4
◇ 7 5 3      W       E       ◇ K Q J 8
♣ A J 9 8 7 6 4    S         ♣ Q 10
```

The two hands were not a perfect fit – was this a message from the stars? However, there were possibilities – and faint heart never won fair contract.

I won the spade continuation with dummy's Ace, discarding a heart from hand. With bated breath I led the ♣Q. It held, but – calamity! – North showed out! How was I to catch K–5–3–2 on my right? My reckless bid was about to bring me grief.

At trick three I tried the ♣10, but South of course was immune to my charms and did not cover, sitting there smirking and guarding his King of trumps. It was now necessary to bring down my trumps to two, the same number as those in the South hand. I ruffed a spade and returned a diamond to the King, then ruffed another spade. With six cards to go, the position was:

```
♠ –                          ♠ K
♡ A 10          N            ♡ K 9 4
◇ 7          W       E       ◇ Q J
♣ A J 9        S             ♣ –
```

Would the hearts be kind? I played the ♡A followed by the ♡K, then ruffed a heart. The moment of truth arrived: I played a diamond to the Queen and, to my relief, South followed. Now it did not matter which of the two remaining cards was led from dummy – the King of trumps was caught.

A trump-reduction coup! Not in the textbooks, but here at the table! Happily I gazed across the table, seeking my partner's admiration.

Alas, this is bridge!

'Bit of a rash bid at pairs, partner', he admonished. 'Good job you were lucky with the trumps!'

HOLIDAY HIGHLIGHTS

BY ROY DEMPSTER

When we look back, most of us can think of holiday highlights. However, what I have in mind here is something rather different from the happy memories that this phrase might bring to mind! *Bridge holiday* highlights are the type that I want to look at. Now, I suspect that a large percentage of readers will never have been on a bridge holiday, and a short description might help to set the scene.

What is a bridge holiday? Well, as the name suggests, it is a holiday with a programme of duplicate bridge extending over the whole period of stay. An afternoon, and then an evening session, is usually the order of the day.

Why would you want to go on a holiday and play bridge? Imagine that you are on a warm, sunny beach, or at the edge of a lake in a beautiful mountain scenery – paradise, if your tastes run that way. The morning and the afternoon pass in a warm relaxed way, and dinner is a fitting climax to the day. But then, after dinner? Mm... If you are young and/or trendy, there is no problem: the nearest disco or club can occupy many an evening. However, if you aren't as young as you once were – or perhaps could never have been described as trendy – how to spend the evenings can be something of a problem. If you are not the sun-bathing, surfing, swimming, sailing, hiking, shopping kind, even the occasional afternoon can be a bore. And if it rains...!

Of course, if there are bridge competitions at your hotel, many happy (well, busy, at least!) hours lie in front of you. Even master points are usually awarded, to satisfy those with such ambitions.

The people who travel on bridge holidays represent all categories of bridge players. Not too many tournament stars go along; after all, they are often too busy chasing around national events at home (and, as a result, are too financially stressed to travel abroad very often). The standard is usually very mixed, and the emphasis tends to be on the social, rather than the viciously competitive side.

As you may have guessed, friendliness is an important factor in the pleasure to be gained from one of these holidays. A nice example of that occurred when North–South had an auction of about seven or eight bids before using Blackwood. The response of 5♣ was a great disappointment to the South player – at least, it was until he realized that it had been West (asleep from the fourth bid of the auction) who had confessed that he had no Aces! Now, 5♣ doubled would have cost somewhere in the region of 2300 points, and so the North player who grinned and said, 'Don't worry, I was going to bid that anyway, so I'll bid it now', really deserved an award for friendliness!

Because the bridge is a little more relaxed than in the Gold Cup, this does not mean that the odd exciting hand never rears its head. In a six-table pairs one afternoon, I (making up the numbers) held the East hand in the diagram:

As dealer at Game All, I opened 2♣ (Precision-style, showing clubs) and I heard Left-Hand Opponent overcall 4♡. Partner, whose system it was, bid 5♣, and North bid 5♡. In a teams competition I would have let sleeping dogs lie, but in a pairs? Anyway, I bid 6♣, South bid 6♡, and, after two

```
Dealer: East     ♠ Q J 10 5 3
Game All         ♡ 7 6 3
                 ◊ Q 10 6
                 ♣ 7 4

♠ 9 7 6                      ♠ A 2
♡ J          ┌─────────┐     ♡ 8 4
◊ 8 7 5 4 2  │    N    │     ◊ K J
♣ A K J 10   │ W     E │     ♣ Q 9 8 6 5 3 2
             │    S    │
             └─────────┘
                 ♠ K 8 4
                 ♡ A K Q 10 9 5 2
                 ◊ A 9 3
                 ♣ –
```

passes, I ended the auction with a double. Partner led the ♣A, and this little exercise in misjudgement cost 1660! Dummy's 5♡ was a vintage holiday-bid, but in view of the holdings in South's hand, North's action brought a huge reward. My partner did not seem to think that a diamond lead was marked on the auction and, to be fair, neither did I!

When you are one of the organizers (and also, heaven help you, the Tournament Director) of one of these events, people tend to expect that you will know better than to push opponents into a slam which they might make. Once these tales have circulated, they tend to ensure that any subsequent lectures and seminars are rather poorly attended!

Oh, yes – on the above deal, once the opponents have reached 4♡ you are in for a poor result: 3♡ was the most common contract, with 5♣ (undoubled) coming next.

I have been asked if many instances of brilliant declarer play, squeezes, endplays, etc., ever occur on bridge holidays. They do – but holiday bridge is really about doing what you enjoy in a location of your choice and in congenial company. The tricky stuff can be concocted on the plane home – and it usually is!

THE 1993 LADY MILNE TROPHY

BY MORAG MALCOLM

During the first weekend in June each year, teams of women representing England, Wales, Northern Ireland and Scotland compete for the Lady Milne Trophy.

Last year the event was held in Nottingham, and Scotland emerged as the winners. This year, it was Scotland's turn to host the event. The venue chosen was the Inchyra Grange Hotel, near Falkirk. Could this be Scotland's year again? They were on home ground and therefore had more supporters, as well as a fine hotel with swimming pool and other leisure facilities (though not much leisure time!), beautiful sunny weather, not to mention – or so it seemed – the help of the English. Their team had no Nicola Smith, no Pat Davies, no Sandra Landy, no Michele Handley – even though last year's captain, Mark Horton, was still there, and Heather Dhondy and Sally Dunsby retained their position. The superstars had been replaced by Chris Duckworth and Jane Sutcliffe, with Carole Kelly and Sandy Davies.

Did they do England proud? They certainly did, by finishing 40 VPs ahead of the second-placed team, the final scores being:

England	215 VPs
Scotland	175 VPs
Northern Ireland	161 VPs
Wales	156 VPs

The winners' score must have pleased the English selectors, who chose the first, second, and third pairs from the English trials.

What about the other teams? Wales – I can't fathom! Last year, they won the first seven matches and then lost the rest. This year, they began by defeating both Scotland and England by 21–9, then faded! They were still in second place with three matches to go, but lost them all.

Northern Ireland were whitewashed by England, but then went through the next ten matches quite well. They did not have any big wins, but their losses were by a few IMPs only. They hoisted themselves into third place by defeating Wales in the last match by 19–11.

Just as last year, Scotland started badly, losing the first three matches, then a good spell followed. On Sunday morning they were in third position, but a grand fighting finish (three wins, including a 23–7 against England) brought them up to second place. Scotland will have to practise their sprint-starts for next year!

I have gone through all the hands, as well as watching them being played. Most of them were played in the same contracts, with the lead either breaking the contract or giving an overtrick. More often than not, it was a mistake by the declarer or the defence which caused the swing. The hands were not computer-dealt, and there were not many swingy ones. Here is one which interested me:

```
Dealer: East                    ♠ J 10 9 5 2
Game All                        ♡ 10 9 5 4
                                ◇ Q J
                                ♣ 7 5
         ♠ K 3                              ♠ A Q 8 4
         ♡ Q J 8 6 3 2         N            ♡ —
         ◇ A 9 8 7 4       W        E       ◇ 10 5
         ♣ —                   S            ♣ K J 10 9 8 6 2
                                ♠ 7 6
                                ♡ A K 7
                                ◇ K 6 3 2
                                ♣ A Q 4 3
```

At all tables, East opened the bidding with 1♣, and South overcalled 1NT. What should West do now? If West doubles, should North bid 2♠? If so, will East double, or bid 3♣? When, or if, this is doubled by South, should West stand the double? Who will get it right? Will South get out in safety, or will East–West land into trouble?

Try it out with your partner, and discuss the various bids. Then try and play the hand in 4♣ as East, on the lead of the ♡A. This contract can be made: can you make it?

BLIND MAN'S BUFF

BY MAUREEN DENNISON

Playing teams, it is very disconcerting to come back to your table and find team-mates waving, pleased to have scored the odd 700 points on a board where you collected plus 790 for a wonderful result. This happened to me on the following hand, which looks as though it would be a straight battle in the bidding. A 5♠ contract poses no problems to East–West, and North–South have a good sacrifice in 6♡. It might take you a long time to guess what really happened at the table!

I was playing with three other women in the Swiss Teams at the Iceland Congress, and this board saved a vital match. I opened 1♡ with the South hand, West doubled, and partner raised to 4♡. East didn't feel like coming in over that – and who can blame him? – and the bid came round to West, who doubled again. East still didn't feel like coming in!

Dealer: South
Game All

	♠ 10 8 4	
	♡ A J 8 7 6 5	
	◊ 3	
	♣ J 4 3	
♠ K Q 6 3	N	♠ J 9 7 5 2
♡ –	W E	♡ Q 9
◊ K Q 7 4	S	◊ 10 8 6 5 2
♣ A K 10 5 2		♣ 7
	♠ A	
	♡ K 10 4 3 2	
	◊ A J 9	
	♣ Q 9 8 6	

This time he was not blameless, but it was all to my advantage.

I played in 4♡ doubled. After the lead of the ♣A, the ♣K continuation, and a third club ruffed by East, I claimed my ten tricks and plus 790.

At the other table the first two bids were the same. North, however, bid 4◊, which showed a heart fit and a diamond shortage. East was Ilina Kjartansdottir, and she doubled North's bid. South bid 4♡ and now West, Hulda Hjalmarsdottir, bid 5◊! South saw fit to double this, but this action merely helped declarer to judge the trump suit correctly and make her contract for plus 750!

When someone commented that perhaps East–West could have mentioned their spade suit, Hulda retorted, 'A spade contract would not be doubled!'

THE FIRST OF THREE

BY RICHARD WHEEN

This is the first of three double-dummy problems. For those not in the know, these are problems where, with sight of all four hands, you have to play so as to make the prescribed number of tricks against any defence by the opposition.

The first two problems are classic double-dummy problems, the one below being easier than the second (on page 122); the third (on page 207) is rather different – and, as you will see, rather harder.

North is on lead with hearts as trumps. How are North–South to make all the remaining tricks against any defence?

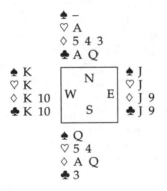

```
                    ♠ –
                    ♡ A
                    ◇ 5 4 3
                    ♣ A Q
      ♠ K          ┌─────────┐      ♠ J
      ♡ K          │    N    │      ♡ J
      ◇ K 10       │ W     E │      ◇ J 9
      ♣ K 10       │    S    │      ♣ J 9
                    └─────────┘
                    ♠ Q
                    ♡ 5 4
                    ◇ A Q
                    ♣ 3
```

Solution on page 213.

AT THE RAINBOW'S END

BY SIMON AINGER

It is impossible not to like Plum Grenville, but he is no dispenser of largesse. And, since we all know that there is no such thing as a free lunch, I ought to have been on my guard. But I'd accepted the invitation before the favour was requested, and it did not sound unduly onerous: since I was the only person he knew who played bridge, would I partner his uncle in a game? The lunch was partly to recompense, but mainly to brief, and the first qualm hit the stomach only after I suggested that he bring along the uncle in question.

'Best not', was the ominous reply.

To appreciate the sadness of this story, you need to understand Plum's circumstances. Had his father been alive, the progress of his only son would have been a sad disappointment. Christened Pelham Charles Scott, his career had started at the font and gone downhill. 'Pelham' was chosen to give him a head-start towards the higher echelons of the legal or diplomatic ranks – Sir Pelham Grenville had a certain ring of inevitability – and the addition of the two further initials was vital for his father's vision of P.C.S. Grenville on the score-card as first wicket down for England in the interim. On the day Pelham was born, in June 1938, one D.C.S. Compton scored 102 against Australia. Plum, however, worked for the Gas Board at a salary which barely serviced mortgage and family. As for the cricket, early promise as a leg spinner at club level was killed by the invasion of leagues and limited overs.

A few years back, however, and unknown to his friends, into Plum's financially precarious life there appeared a rainbow in the form of a long-lost and highly-eccentric uncle, who demanded to be called 'The Captain'. The elder brother of Plum's father had gone away to war and simply disappeared. It was assumed that he had been lost in action; but he had survived, gone to America, made a fortune and decided to spend it going hither and thither on cruise ships. This was no urge to see the world, since the Captain never went ashore in port. On board he played bridge and survived exclusively on a diet of white fish and champagne. His shock re-entry into Plum's life came via a telephone call from Southampton. Plum drove down to meet him and, in the process, satisfied himself of his authenticity. Thereafter there came further irregular summonses to partake of a plate of poached turbot and a glass or two of Bollinger. Plum, with intuition but no evidence, was convinced that his uncle had deserted during the war, made his money by nefarious means, and finally contacted his nephew through the international Mafia. He judged it prudent not to delve too deeply. There must be a pot of gold, and its origin was unimportant; what was vital was its ultimate home. Matters progressed when his uncle decided that he wanted to die on dry land and in his mother country. Plum happily offered bed and board while the old boy pursued his announced intention of looking for a property to buy.

All this I learnt with fascination and trepidation during the arranged lunch. The Captain was now ensconced in the spare room, content to absorb *Vin de Pays* if provided in adequate quantity, but missing his bridge. The local club was happy to accept visitors, but only as a pair. Plum was, as ever, eager to please, and I was required to play my part.

Despite contemplating the acquisition of strategic contagious diseases, I honoured the arrangement and the experience was not as bad as I had feared. There was no problem in locating the Captain: roll-neck sweater, reefer jacket and a rolling gait gained, no doubt, from years of negotiating sloping decks without spilling the glass.

We tried to agree a system of sorts.

'I usually open a spade if I get a chance', said the Captain.

'What does that show?' I asked.

'Thirteen cards', he replied. 'Gets the bidding to a more exciting level and tends to confuse the enemy.'

I managed to persuade him that this might cause some problems, and we settled on a strong no-trump, forcing twos, and Blackwood. Not that it mattered very much: every time we started a bidding sequence, the Captain always seemed to end up in 3NT, but he played the hands well and things did not go too far adrift.

But the final hand had me worried:

```
Dealer: South    ♠ J 7
N/S Vul          ♡ 6 3
                 ◇ K Q J 10 4
                 ♣ J 7 6 5

♠ K 9 5 4              ┌──────────┐   ♠ A Q 10 3 2
♡ A 9 7 5 2            │    N     │   ♡ Q J 10 8
◇ 9 8 6                │ W     E  │   ◇ 5 2
♣ 9                    │    S     │   ♣ 10 8
                       └──────────┘

                 ♠ 8 6
                 ♡ K 4
                 ◇ A 7 3
                 ♣ A K Q 4 3 2
```

The Captain was sitting South, and I suppose temptation finally overcame discretion. He opened 1♠. I replied 2◊ and the Captain bid the inevitable 3NT. The play was soon over: the ♡5 was led, and twelve tricks were wrapped up. I quickly recorded our top, muttered about the late hour and trains to catch, grabbed the Captain by the arm and hustled him out of the door before the inquest could begin. We shook hands and departed in opposite directions. I reeled and he rolled, and we were never to meet again.

It was quite some while before I made contact with Plum again. Business took me out of the country and, anyway, I was nervous that I might get involved again. But eventually I did telephone him.

'How's the Captain?' I asked.

'Dead', said Plum.

I was unsure whether he was imparting good news or bad news. The Captain, it transpired, had become not just a welcomed member of the bridge club, but a big hit with the ladies at the afternoon rubber sessions. Mornings in bed, afternoons playing bridge, and evenings drinking had become the Captain's routine. Missing from this itinerary was house-hunting. Eventually Plum had to tackle the problem.

'Good news', the Captain announced. 'Soon to be gone. Getting married next week. Lovely girl that I met at the bridge club.'

The rainbow had vanished – and with it the pot of gold now destined for the buxom, flame-haired bride-to-be. The marriage took place, but the honeymoon was brief: the Captain dropped dead two days into it. The pot of gold? That, alas, had long been scoured and the Captain, like his nephew, had been looking out for the main chance.

'Died happy, I suppose', said Plum, wistful and melancholic.

THE INVISIBLE RUFF

BY PATRICK JOURDAIN

The International Bridge Press Association is a club with four hundred of the world's journalists as members. As Editor of its monthly Bulletin I receive excellent hands from around the world, and one of the most prolific correspondents is a Romanian, Vlad Racoviceanu. This deal, submitted from their Bridge Festival in Bucharest, is a most deceptive one:

Dealer: East
N/S Vul

```
                                  ♠ 8 2
                                  ♡ 2
                                  ◊ A K Q J 4
                                  ♣ A Q J 10 9
            ♠ 10                            ♠ K Q J 9
            ♡ Q 10 9 7 5 3    N            ♡ A K J
            ◊ 10 8 2        W     E        ◊ 7 6
            ♣ 6 5 4            S            ♣ K 8 7 3
                                  ♠ A 7 6 5 4 3
                                  ♡ 8 6 4
                                  ◊ 9 5 3
                                  ♣ 2
```

South	West	North	East
			1NT (a)
NB	2◊ (b)	Dbl (c)	2♡
3◊	NB	5◊	Dbl
End			

(a) 15–17.
(b) Transfer.
(c) 12+ High-Card Points.

The bidding was a little complicated, but North–South ended in the best contract of 5◊, though the declarer proved to be South, who had the shorter trump holding.

Look at the diagram and count South's tricks. He has five trumps, four clubs, and the ♠A. That adds up to ten. His eleventh trick was a ruff, but see if you can guess which card the declarer, Imre Pal, ruffed to make his contract.

Pal won the spade lead and immediately began with ♣A–Q. East wisely did not cover (or South's ruff becomes an easy source of the eleventh trick). Pal, foreseeing the danger of a late over-ruff, discarded a *heart* from his hand.

East refused to cover the next club, and a second heart went away. When the fourth club was led, East finally covered. If Pal ruffs this, he is overruffed ... but Pal discarded his last heart, a classic loser-on-loser play that secured the contract.

He was unable to make a club ruff, but had disposed of all three hearts from the South hand. His eleventh trick came from ruffing North's ♡2!

If West had led a heart and East had withheld the ♣K as he did, then 5◇ would have been defeated. And the invisible ruff would not have shown its face.

JOHNNY RAW'S CONVENTION CARD

One night Johnny Raw, a shy 20-year old from Surrey, summoned up his courage and his favourite partner, and went to play duplicate at a strong Berkshire club. Our heroes' results on the first few rounds were rather poor, but they were just about settling down when the movement pitted them against the club's stars – two men who took the game very seriously.

On the first board, Johnny opened 2♠ and his partner alerted. LHO picked up Johnny's convention card, waved away with an impatient hand any explanation Johnny's partner was about to proffer, and studied the card carefully. Finally, he made a bid.

'So that's where I left it!' exclaimed a flustered lady. With a relieved smile she picked up the convention card that had been so thoroughly perused, and went back to sit at the next table.

NIL DESPERANDUM!

BY KEN HAYTON

You are sitting South in a county league match with a good and reliable partner. Indeed you are regarded – rightly or wrongly – as the pair least likely to let down the rest of the team. Furthermore, that team is so engaged in a life-or-death struggle to avoid relegation that the pressure in this last match is definitely on – and it is intensified when the hand below is picked up:

South
♠ A K J 10 9 7 6
♡ –
◇ A K 8 6 2
♣ A

Although it is twenty years since you held a hand as good as this, you can remember the system and open 2♣. Partner (good and reliable!) gives a positive response of 2♡ from the South seat, and you continue with an unhurried 2♠. Partner now bids 3♠, and it is time to take stock.

Clearly things are looking good, even exciting, so a cue-bid of 4♣ seems to be in order.

Partner cue-bids 4♡ – not unexpected, and not particularly helpful. However, we press on with 5♣, and partner bids 5♡. Having shown eight, or probably nine, cards in the major suits, and the ♡A–K, the grand looks to be odds-on, and you bid it with some confidence. The ♣K is led, and your good, reliable partner puts down the following:

North
♠ Q 5 4 2
♡ A K J 9 2
◇ 9 4 3
♣ 6

There is everything he claimed to have held, and more: a singleton. But, much against the odds, it is the wrong singleton. What is worse is the fact that your beautiful hand is too good, and there is only one entry to dummy via the ♠Q. Had dummy held the ♠8, or you the ♠3, there would have been a fighting chance of setting up a third discard in the heart suit, but to bring down the ♡Q in two is a forlorn hope. There is but one thing in your favour. The bidding has concealed your long diamond suit, and it appears that your best chance might be the old confidence trick of a false squeeze. It worked! Not a surprise to you, I realize, but let us see how it worked.

You win the opening lead with your ♣A, play ♠A–K, East showing a void, and then enter dummy via the ♠Q. Everybody has been discarding clubs, so you grit your teeth and return to hand with a spade,

71

cutting yourself off for ever from those lovely heart honours. Now you play three more rounds of spades and, with the increasing discomfiture on East's face, your hopes rise. On the last spade he reluctantly discards a diamond, and the contract is yours. It is difficult to blame East for his wrong decision if you consider the full deal:

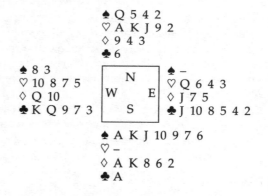

```
                ♠ Q 5 4 2
                ♡ A K J 9 2
                ◇ 9 4 3
                ♣ 6
  ♠ 8 3                          ♠ –
  ♡ 10 8 7 5        N            ♡ Q 6 4 3
  ◇ Q 10        W       E        ◇ J 7 5
  ♣ K Q 9 7 3       S            ♣ J 10 8 5 4 2
                ♠ A K J 10 9 7 6
                ♡ –
                ◇ A K 8 6 2
                ♣ A
```

Partner's club discards and declarer's failure to ruff a club have made the distribution of that suit clear, but what about the others? It is hard to imagine that declarer would have abandoned his heart honours – and so he is thought to hold at least one heart, and be striving for a squeeze in the red suits. Partner has followed to trumps twice, discarded all his clubs, and at trick eight he has let go of a heart. The end position which you face with a discard to find is shown below:

```
♠ –
♡ A K J 9
◇ 9
♣ –
```

```
          ♠ –
          ♡ Q 6 4
          ◇ J 7 5
          ♣ –
```

How, in all honesty, would you have played?

Could we find West guilty, then? If you consider his hand carefully, you will see that he could have discarded in a way which would have left his partner with no difficulty – but would you have found that defence? (If you can't, see below!)

West should discard four hearts!

A PRINCIPLE IN DEFENCE

BY G C H FOX

There are many players who openly boast that they have never read a bridge book in their life. Such players might well go wrong in the situation that arose on this hand from a congress pairs tournament. It illustrates a principle that has been written up in books on play and defence, and those who have benefited from reading would be likely to recognize the position:

```
Dealer: South              ♠ 4 3
Love All                   ♡ A K 10 9 5
                           ◇ Q 7 3
                           ♣ 6 5 3
        ♠ A 9 8 6 5    ┌─────────┐   ♠ Q J 7
        ♡ 8 7 3        │    N    │   ♡ J 6 4
        ◇ 10 9 2       │  W   E  │   ◇ J 8 6 4
        ♣ K Q          │    S    │   ♣ 10 8 2
                       └─────────┘
                           ♠ K 10 2
                           ♡ Q 2
                           ◇ A K 5
                           ♣ A J 9 7 4
```

The popular contract was 3NT played by South, making ten tricks after a spade lead from West. A few Souths played successfully in 4♡, and others in the inferior contract of 5♣.

At one table West started with the ♠A against 5♣, and continued with the ♠6 to the ♠J and ♠K. South's problem is to avoid losing two tricks in trumps. He enters dummy by ruffing the ♠10 and leads the ♣6, on which East follows with the ♣2, and the ♣9 loses to the ♣Q. It is correct to play the ♣9 on the first round, as it stands to gain if East holds the ♣10 plus either the ♣K or the ♣Q, whereas to play the ♣J only succeeds if East holds both the ♣K and the ♣Q. In other words, playing the ♣9 is finessing against one card, the ♣10, rather than two, the ♣K and ♣Q.

After regaining the lead with the ◇Q, the ♣3 is led and East follows with the ♣8. What should South play? He must play the ♣A and hope that the ♣K is bare with West. If he finesses the ♣J and it wins, he must still lose a club, as East will hold ♣K–10–8–2. So much for declarer's play.

On the second club lead East must play the ♣10. Now, in all probability, South will finesse the ♣J and lose. This is logical, as the play to the first two rounds suggests East's holding to be ♣K–10–2 and West's ♣Q–8. The principle in defence can be stated thus: providing it is not likely to cost a certain trick, a defender should always play a card which he is known to hold. Once the ♣9 drew either the ♣K or the ♣Q, East was known to hold the ♣10.

Here is another example:

♠ K 9 6 4

♠ 8 3 2 | N W E S | ♠ Q 10 5

♠ A J 7

South leads the ♠4 from the table and finesses the ♠J. He follows with the ♠A and East must play the ♠Q – the card which he is known to hold. Now when South leads the ♠7 and West follows with the ♠8, he must guess whether to play the ♠K or the ♠9 from dummy.

NOVICE CLUB

'It's a top for us!'
  'No, it's a top for us!'
  'Oh, sorry, I remember: we were North–South yesterday!'

Merle Jarrett

CROSSING ALTERNATE BRIDGES

BY N E WOOD

Apart from the well-known and well-used Bridge, there are a number of alternatives. These range from games for three players – nice if you're missing a fourth – to types of Bridges designed to carry five players (or even more). Here are seven alternatives:

Bridge(s) for Three Players

The first alternative has a rather blood-thirsty name:

CUTTHROAT. For this game, four hands are dealt in the normal way, 'dummy' remaining face down. Bidding follows in the normal way (except for the fact that each player bids on the basis of his own hand only), and eventually declarer plays the dummy hand which is now turned face up. The scoring follows normal rubber bridge rules. There are no partnerships, but if declarer's bid is defeated, both opponents score above the line.

TOWIE is a somewhat more complex variation. After the deal, six of dummy's cards are turned face up, then the bidding takes place as described above – but made more interesting by the six faced cards. Declarer plays the dummy hand as in Cutthroat Bridge. However, if the contract is not enough for game (the score being less than 100), the hand is re-dealt as follows: each player sorts his hand into suits (if this has not been done already), dealer doing the same for the dummy hand which is checked by the other players. The dealer then places his own hand face down and stacks the other cards on top of them, in this order: Left-Hand Opponent, Dummy, Right-Hand Opponent. After a cut the deck is dealt out in batches of 5–5–3 cards. Dealer then shuffles the dummy hand and turns six cards face up. Bidding then re-starts.

NINETY-NINE is an interesting game that has been designed for three players, with some very nice twists. A short pack of 37 cards is used (from the Ace down to the 6 in each suit, plus a Joker). Each player is dealt twelve cards and the last card is turned face up to establish trumps for the deal; if this card is the Joker or a Nine, the deal is played in no-trumps.

The Joker in a player's hand takes on the identity of the faced card, and it is played as if it were that card.

The bidding method is quite clever: each player discards three cards – each club discarded counts as a bid of three tricks, each heart as two tricks, each spade as one trick, and each diamond no tricks. The object is to score exactly the number of tricks bid. Bonus points are given if a player 'declares' his bid, i.e. plays the hand with his bid cards face up (only one player may so declare his bid in a deal). A player can also 'reveal' his hand: in this case, he places his bid cards face up, and also plays his hand face up.

The scoring is as follows: 1 point per trick (regardless of bid), 30 points if only one player has made his bid, 20 each if two succeed, and 10 each if all three succeed (depending on the bids, this is quite possible). The bonus for a declared bid is 30 points, and for a revealed hand it is 60. The winner of the game is the player with the highest score after nine deals.

Bridge(s) for Four Players

FIVE-SUIT BRIDGE is a normal game with an extra suit (in Britain the suit was green and was called 'Crowns', while in the USA it was blue and named 'Eagles') ranking above spades. This version was apparently popular in the 1930s. If anyone is interested in trying out this game, but lacks the special pack of cards, use a suit from another pack with a different face pattern.

BRINT uses a different scoring system. Below the line, each trick score ten times the value of the contract (thus 1X = 10). Game equals 500 below the line. The bonuses are: 1000 for game, 200 for rubber, 1000 for twelve tricks (plus 500 if they were bid), 2000 for thirteen tricks (plus 1000 if they were bid), and one hundred times the trick value per under-trick. Other rules remain standard.

VINT is an ancestor of Bridge, where the suits rank as follows (low to high); spades, clubs, diamonds, hearts, no-trumps. The contract is established after *eight* passes, and scoring is the same as described under Brint above.

JUNGLE BRIDGE can be played by up to seven players. In the first deal of a game, each player receives one card, in the second two cards, and so on; the number of players thus dictates the number of deals in a game. As in Ninety-nine, the object is to score exactly the number of tricks you bid. After the deal, the next card is turned up to establish trumps. Scoring: each player making his bid scores his bid plus 10. Nothing else scores. Again as in Ninety-nine, more than one player can make his bid – except, of course, in the first deal.

There you have it – an interesting set of different Bridges. I hope you enjoy them!

BIDDING BOXES

At the first evening of using Bidding Boxes, East was searching through the bids at the end of an auction that had not gone well. When asked, 'What are you looking for?', East replied, 'The one which says S--T!'

(from the NCBA newsletter)

THE REVERSE AUCTION

BY RON HEATH

North had the perfect Gambling 3NT opening hand, based on an eight-card solid club suit, but in his excitement he actually called 4NT. No bid from East.

South duly alerted and explained – quite correctly – that his partner was asking him to name his Ace(s). Being rather proud that he had remembered this wonderful once-in-a-lifetime convention, he also was overcome with excitement and, looking at the ◊A, replied 4◊.

East–West had never heard of this convention, and were so stunned at the high level of bridge by their opponents that they passed in a trance. North – who was unaware of his original error – was much perplexed by the explanation and subsequent bid; but he woke up to his duties as a correct and ethical player and attempted to work out what he should now bid as if he had never heard his partner's explanation. No one could question a natural bid of his clubs, so he did – at the four level!

Everyone was now confused, and there followed three no-bids. East thought that he was on lead, but was wise enough to ask for a review. North's version was, of course, not the same as the others', so the Director was called to hear the Reverse Auction agreed by the other three players. Law 27A was the one to consult: 'Any insufficient bid may be accepted (treated as legal) at the option of the offender's left-hand opponent. It is accepted if that player calls.'

In each case of the insufficient bid, the next player had said no bid, i.e. a call, thus accepting the bid. The full recap was: 4NT – NB – 4◊ – NB – 4♣ – NB – NB – NB!

JUST ANOTHER DUPLICATE

BY SPOIL NULAW

Saturday evening at the He-Man Bridge Club is a session for experienced players, vying for a kitty worth up to £100. The director for the night, Ramnon, and his wife and partner Nojane, were playing East–West on this board, opposite Evil-lyn (South) and that well-known McEnroe of the international bridge world, Skeletor (North).

Dealer: East
Love All

	♠ 10 3
	♡ A Q 10 8 6
	◊ J 9 7 6
	♣ 6 2

North hand:
- ♠ 10 3
- ♡ A Q 10 8 6
- ◊ J 9 7 6
- ♣ 6 2

West hand:
- ♠ Q 4 2
- ♡ 9 4
- ◊ A 8 4
- ♣ K J 10 5 4

East hand:
- ♠ −
- ♡ K 7 3 2
- ◊ Q 10 5 3
- ♣ A Q 8 7 3

South hand:
- ♠ A K J 9 8 7 6 5
- ♡ J 5
- ◊ K 2
- ♣ 9

South	West	North	East
			NB
1♠	2♣	Dbl (a)	3♣
4♠	NB (b)	NB	5♣
? (c)			

(a) Alerted as showing the other two suits.
(b) After an allegedly long hesitation.
(c) What next?

At this point South, Evil-lyn, objected to the hesitation rather than reserving her rights, and Director Ramnon sitting West maintained that he was a player of long experience and entitled to think after the 'Stop, 4♠' for up to ten seconds if he wanted to. Nojane, East, sprang to her partner's defence asking if the opponents thought they were cheating or something! All this was too much for North and, true to form, Skeletor threw a wobbly – or rather, threw a side table narrowly missing the lady on the table opposite. Next came the actual board. 'I never knew duplicate boards to be so aerodynamic', remarked an elderly gentleman at Table One, as the object in question whistled past his right ear.

Funny? Not really. Evil-lyn was over eight months pregnant and was extremely distressed. Nevertheless, she managed to calm her partner down, he apologized, and the auction continued – the room in a deadly hush:

South	West	North	East
			NB
1♠	2♣	Dbl	3♣
4♠	NB	NB	5♣
5♠	Dbl	End	

South bid 5♠, West doubled, and that was the final contract – and the final straw for North. He walked out, desperately trying to take the lobby door off its hinges as he went. Then he came back to have another go, moving the fruit machine (about a ton or so in weight), with the lobby door bending a curtain rail for good measure. Then he turned his attention to the Director – and that's when the evening cabaret came to a close.

The point of real bridge interest in this story is that 5♠ doubled goes two or three off, and one pair actually made 5♣ plus one.

All those applying for the job of Tournament Director should queue up outside the He-Man club every Saturday night at 7.45 p.m. Skeletor will not be there.

This account is not intended to be strictly accurate. The names of the author, characters and venue have been changed.

IT HAPPENED IN HANTS

After a long, keenly-fought match which ended in a draw, Dave Henbrey was heard to comment: 'It was carnage. We cut ourselves to ribbons!'

(from The Kibitzer)

BETTER THAN NONE

BY DAVE HUGGETT

There is nothing more infuriating than to have bid to a contract which appears to have no play whatsoever, but it is in these situations that an expert declarer can sometimes find a slim hope denied to lesser mortals.

Declarer on this hand from the final of a pairs competition was just such a player, so see if you can emulate his performance and give yourself a chance to make 6♡ as South on the lead of the ♠K:

♠ A 7 3
♡ 8 7 6 4 2   Solution on page 213.
◊ 3
♣ K Q J 8

```
     N
  W     E
     S
```

♠ 8
♡ Q J 10 9 5
◊ A K Q J 7
♣ A 4

AN OBVIOUS BID

East: 'What was your 6♣ bid, partner?'
West: 'Well, it was a slam-try, wasn't it?'

(from the NCBA newsletter)

NEW YORK'S FINEST

BY TONY GORDON

Christine Cagney glanced impatiently at her watch. It seemed that her partner, Mary Beth Lacey, was being even more careful than usual in her play of the hand. 'Maybe I'm unfairly comparing Mary Beth with Charlie', she thought to herself. There was no denying that her father was quicker at analysing and playing a hand than most bridge players she had come across. 'The sooner the hand is over, the sooner I can have a drink', he used to say to her, jokingly. Come to think of it, if she hadn't told Lt. Samuels that she and Charlie used to play regularly with Mary Beth and Harvey Lacey, she wouldn't have found herself playing in the annual inter-precinct Swiss Teams. They were currently playing the last board of the first match, and she could see the familiar figure of the Lieutenant hovering outside the playing area waiting for them to finish. This was the hand that was causing problems for Mary Beth:

Dealer: South
Love All

	♠ 7 6 5	
	♡ A 9 2	
	◇ K 6 5 4 2	
	♣ J 3	
♠ J 10 9 8	N	♠ K Q 4 3
♡ K 10 4 3	W E	♡ J 8 5
◇ J 10 9 7	S	◇ 3
♣ 4		♣ A 10 8 5 2
	♠ A 2	
	♡ Q 7 6	
	◇ A Q 8	
	♣ K Q 9 7 6	

South	West	North	East
1♣	NB	1◇	NB
2NT	NB	3NT	End

The opening lead had been the ♠J. Hoping that the suit was breaking 4–4, Mary Beth had won with the ♠A and led a club towards the Jack. East had taken his Ace, cashed two high spades, and then played his last spade. Mary Beth had discarded hearts from both hands on the spades and won West's ◇J switch with the ◇A. However, when East discarded a heart on the ◇Q, her nine tricks had suddenly shrunk to seven. This was the position as Mary Beth pondered her next move:

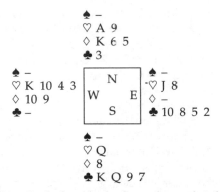

```
              ♠ -
              ♡ A 9
              ◇ K 6 5
              ♣ 3
   ♠ -                      ♠ -
   ♡ K 10 4 3      N        ♡ J 8
   ◇ 10 9      W      E     ◇ -
   ♣ -             S        ♣ 10 8 5 2
              ♠ -
              ♡ Q
              ◇ 8
              ♣ K Q 9 7
```

It seemed to Mary Beth that she had to rely on the club suit for four tricks, but how likely was it that the suit was breaking 3–3? If that was the case, East would have had a 4–5–1–3 shape with sufficient values (♣A and ♠K–Q, so far) to have made a take-out double after North's response. East's silence suggested instead that he had club length rather than heart length and that, consequently, the correct play was to finesse against the ♣10. South therefore crossed to dummy's ◇K, East discarding another heart, and finessed the ♣9. The operation was successful, but West's heart discard meant that declarer was still one trick short. However, it suddenly occurred to her that, as East guarded clubs and West guarded diamonds, the elements of a double squeeze were present. She did a quick recap: East, who had started with three hearts, had been reduced to only one heart by the play of the top diamonds; West, who had started with four hearts, had discarded one on the ♣9, and would be squeezed in the red suits when she played her two winning clubs. Hardly able to contain her excitement, she cashed the ♣K, throwing a diamond from dummy as West threw a heart. The ♣Q forced West to discard another heart as dummy's last diamond went away leaving the ♡A and ♡9 to take the last two tricks.

Flushed with success, Mary Beth turned to Christine for approval, but found her partner deep in thought. 'Christine', she implored, 'you can't spend the entire tournament wondering why David Keeler hasn't phoned you'.

'Give me a break, Mary Beth', retorted Christine, 'I was simply working out whether West should have been smart enough to break up the squeeze by playing the ♡K instead of the ◇J. Of course, that doesn't detract from your fine play', she added quickly. Her vanity satisfied, Mary Beth turned away and began checking the scores with her opponents.

Left to her deliberations, Christine concluded that West had indeed erred by not playing the ♡K. It should have been clear that as long as declarer had three club winners, the contract could always be made on a squeeze. If declarer had started with five clubs and three hearts, there would be a double squeeze unless dummy's ♡A entry was knocked out. If declarer had started with only four clubs and a four-card heart suit that she had concealed during the bidding, the third club winner would squeeze West in the red suits as South was marked with the ♡Q. In the latter case, the play of the ♡K would do no more than hasten his demise. On the other hand, if declarer had only two club winners, she would have only seven tricks – and, even if the ♡K switch resented her with an eighth, she had nowhere to go for her ninth trick.

Christine anxiously looked over to the other table where her teammates, Marcus Petrie, sitting East, and Victor Isbecki, sitting West, were engaged in animated conversation. 'Victor is probably defending his optimistic bidding', she thought, but immediately took comfort in the fact that the ♡K was exactly the kind of play that would appeal to his flamboyant nature.

It wasn't long before Petrie and Isbecki came over to compare scores, and Christine could see Lt. Samuels making his way towards their table. The match had been very close and everything hinged on the last hand. It transpired that Petrie and Isbecki had defeated the 3NT contract by one trick, and as a result they had won the match by 7 IMPs.

'I could hug you, Victor', enthused Christine, 'I knew you would break up the squeeze'.

Although Isbecki was sorely tempted to take advantage of Christine's offer, he had to concede that Petrie deserved all the credit. 'But I would have found the killing defence if the need had arisen', he hastened to reassure her.

Christine looked quizzically at Petrie. 'It's quite simple, really', he said modestly. 'When declarer played to dummy's ♣J, I ducked. I thought it would be a good idea to let declarer commit himself in clubs at an early stage. Since he thought he needed only two club tricks, he continued with a club to the King, but when diamonds failed to break he had no fallback position'.

By now, the Lieutenant had arrived at the table. 'I'm glad you have made a reasonable start', he said. 'The 14th precinct has a poor record in this event, and I bet Sgt. Coleman that we would finish in the top ten this year. You won't let me down, will you?'

'No, Lieutenant', they chorused together.

HOLIDAY FUN

BY PAUL HACKETT

Looking back on my bridge holidays, I can remember many amusing incidents. A few stand out in my mind.

A Tale of Cornflakes

Lulu St George was with my group on the island of Gaspe Grande in Trinidad, and was told that there were no cornflakes. 'Do not worry, sir', said the head waiter, 'I will send someone to the mainland to get some.' So Lulu sat in the sun, and watched the speedboat disappear over the horizon. About twenty minutes later, the man reappeared triumphantly with one packet of cornflakes. When this failed to appear at the breakfast table, Lulu called over the waiter and asked for his cornflakes. 'Sorry, sir', he was told again, 'no cornflakes.'

At this point Lulu took the waiter into the kitchen and pointed out the recently arrived packet.

'Ah!' said the waiter. 'Sorry – no milk!'

A Near Lynching

Hanna Warner was one of the group of players who had joined me for the Cino Del Duca tournament in Paris. On our return, the air pilots went on strike and our party was re-routed via Brussels, where there were about three hundred people waiting to board the last plane back to London. I asked my group to follow me when my name was called, and Hanna was in the middle of the group. When she got to the barrier, she said in a voice which the whole room could hear: 'I haven't got a ticket!'

We nearly got lynched.

A Helpful Partner

One of my regular partners had a few drinks too many, and fell off his chair. His partner came round, apologized to the opponents, helped his friend back in his chair, and announced: 'Just straightening the dummy!'

FLAT BOARD

BY SALLY HORTON

Very often, even at the highest level, careless declarer play goes unpunished. On the following deal, taken from a recent international event, I gaily embarked on a line of play with no clear plan in mind.

As South, I opened a 14–16 1NT, and in due course became declarer in 4♠. I do sometimes play hands well, I promise, but on this occasion I certainly did not give the hand enough thought.

Dealer: South
Game All

	♠ K 9 4 2	
	♡ K 10 7 6	
	◇ K J 4	
	♣ 6 2	

♠ Q J		♠ 8 7 5
♡ J 9 5	N	♡ Q 8 4 3
◇ 9 7 6 3	W　　E	◇ A 10
♣ K Q 10 9	S	♣ J 8 4 3

	♠ A 10 6 3	
	♡ A 2	
	◇ Q 8 5 2	
	♣ A 7 5	

West led the ♣K, which I ducked, and continued with another club, which I won with the Ace. I now played a spade to the King and, being very familiar with the Principle of Restricted Choice, a spade back to the Ten and Jack. West exited with a third club; I ruffed this in dummy and paused to take stock – a few tricks too late! I appeared to have put myself in a position where I needed diamonds to break 3–3. Oh dear! I could probably have done something rather better than this. Never mind, I drew the last trump and West discarded… a diamond. No problems – plus 620. Let's put the cards back in the slot quickly before anyone notices!

In the other room, declarer played rather more intelligently. The play to the first three tricks was the same, but when West played a spade honour on the first round of the suit, she saw no need to commit herself immediately. Instead of playing another spade, she played a heart to the Ace and a diamond to the King. East won with the Ace and returned the ◊10, which declarer won in dummy. Again, declarer saw no pressing need to play trumps, and she played a diamond off the dummy. East chose not to ruff this (it might have been better if she had), so declarer won with the Queen, following with a heart to dummy's King and a heart ruff. She then ruffed her last club in the dummy, and played a heart in this end position:

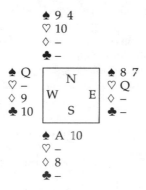

East followed with the ♡Q, and South had to decide what to do.

Do you see what has happened? It is no longer a guess – East has only played one trump so far, and only has two cards left, so it is not possible for trumps to be 4–1! Not that the trump distribution is relevant – all declarer has to do is ruff with the ♠A, and ruff her last diamond with the ♠9 to ensure two out of the last three tricks and her contract.

Well played! Flat board.

EAVESDROPPINGS

'What's your leading style?'
    'Moral Defeat!'

PRESERVE COMMUNICATIONS

BY DANNY ROTH

One of the best aids to bridge memory is the ability to see and recognize a situation from both the declarer's and defenders' point of view. No-trump contracts, in particular, often involve the declarer trying to set up a long suit in dummy while the defenders try to stop him. The golden rule, applicable to *both* sides, is 'Try to lose tricks as early as possible to preserve communications'. Let us look first at the defenders' point of view – take the East seat on this deal:

```
    ♠ 7 4 2
    ♡ 8 5
    ◊ A J 10 9 7 5
    ♣ 6 4
  ┌───────┐      ♠ 8 3
  │   N   │      ♡ K J 7 4
  │ W   E │      ◊ K 6 3
  │   S   │      ♣ K J 5 2
  └───────┘
```

At Love All, South deals and opens 2NT, promising 20–21 points, and North raises to game in 3NT. Partner leads the ♠Q, South's ♠K winning. He now plays the ◊Q to partner's ◊4 and dummy's ◊5. How do you defend?

It is clear that, with five points in dummy and eleven in your hand, South must have all the outstanding honours apart from the ♠J, which is obviously in partner's hand. Thus the contract depends on bringing in that diamond suit for five tricks – to go with the two top spades and the Aces of clubs and hearts, with a finesse in one of those suits being available for an overtrick.

South knows that, if the diamond finesse is right and the suit breaks reasonably, there will be no problem. If it is wrong, however, lack of entries to dummy make it crucial to lose the first round of the suit. East must thwart this plan by ducking the first diamond trick. South is likely to repeat the finesse, hoping for

```
              ♠ 7 4 2
              ♡ 8 5
              ◊ A J 10 9 7 5
              ♣ 6 4
♠ Q J 10 9 5  ┌───────┐  ♠ 8 3
♡ 10 6 2      │   N   │  ♡ K J 7 4
◊ 4 2         │ W   E │  ◊ K 6 3
♣ 10 9 7      │   S   │  ♣ K J 5 2
              └───────┘
              ♠ A K 6
              ♡ A Q 9 3
              ◊ Q 8
              ♣ A Q 8 3
```

the ◇K to be with West. But now East produces the King – and declarer will probably be held to six tricks. Note how *both* sides gain from losing the first trick. The full deal was as shown bottom of page 88.

If East has only a doubleton diamond he must still pluck up the courage to duck – that is the only hope. Provided he does so without hesitation, South will have little reason to refuse the second finesse.

Having seen the idea, you can now try a more difficult example, this time from declarer's point of view. Take the South seat below:

♠ Q 6 4
♡ K Q J 6 3
◇ 9 6 2
♣ 8 4

```
      N
  W       E
      S
```

♠ A K 2
♡ 5 2
◇ A J 4 3
♣ A K 7 5

At Game All, you open 1♣; partner responds 1♡ and you bid 3NT. West leads the ♠J. Counting your tricks, you can see three in spades, two in clubs, and one in diamonds on top, and therefore you need only *three* heart tricks. The first vital point is to win the first trick in hand to preserve the ♠Q as long as possible as your entry to dummy. Now insist on losing the first round of hearts by playing low in both hands. If they return a spade, win again in hand, and play a second heart to an honour. This guarantees three heart tricks and the contract, as long as the suit breaks 3–3 or 4–2, and you have the added bonus of success if East has a stiff ♡A. The full deal is shown below:

You should satisfy yourself of two things. Firstly, if you play a heart to an honour at trick one, East will duck and you will be held to two tricks in the suit. You will then be forced to rely on a friendly diamond split to make your contract. Secondly, that there is no combination of diamonds that will beat you if the defenders switch to that suit on winning the first heart.

♠ Q 6 4
♡ K Q J 6 3
◇ 9 6 2
♣ 8 4

♠ J 10 9 7   ♠ 8 5 3
♡ 8 4   N   ♡ A 10 9 7
◇ K 10 7 5   W   E   ◇ Q 8
♣ J 6 3   S   ♣ Q 10 9 2

♠ A K 2
♡ 5 2
◇ A J 4 3
♣ A K 7 5

DOWN BY THE RIVERSIDE

BY WENDY WENSUM

It was a strange trio that boarded the plane at Gatwick Airport. Following our visit to Spain, my friend Millie and I felt pleasantly at ease as we made our way on our latest venture to an Easter bridge holiday in Rhodes. However, unlike the Spanish trip, my spouse had decided to accompany us this time, on the strict understanding that under no circumstances whatever would he be forced to play bridge. Millie and I agreed willingly, as without doubt he is the most reluctant bridge player the world has ever seen.

Rhodes is a beautiful island, hot and crowded in summer, but at Easter warm and tourist-free. The hotel was situated on the peninsula at the northern end of the island, close to the castle overlooking the ancient harbour once guarded by the Colossus of Rhodes. As Spouse went exploring the town with its museums and art galleries, Millie and I settled down to our first session of bridge.

'Why Rhodes?' I had pondered when Millie first suggested the holiday in early March. The answer now became clear, as the Personable Stranger from the Spanish jaunt approached from the other end of the room. He and Millie were re-acquainted in traditional Mediterranean style, and Millie looked quite flushed as bridge proceeded. I was not surprised to learn that we finished third from the bottom with a measly 44%, whereas the Personable Stranger finished top with a sparkling 67%.

That evening, Spouse took me to his discovery of the afternoon, a delightful *taverna* by an old mosque close to the Turkish quarter within the mediaeval walled town. Millie, the PS, and his partner dined elsewhere, consuming several litres of wine, followed by a few brandies.

On the next day, Millie and I were due to play in the team event with the PS and his partner. Unfortunately, the latter was suffering from the necessity to lie motionless in his darkened room. A substitute partner for the PS had to be found urgently, and Millie eagerly volunteered. This caused another problem, and an emergency solution had to be found.

'No! No! No!' shrieked Spouse, as he was dragged into the bridge room. 'I mean NO!' shouted Spouse as he was sat down unceremoniously at the bridge table. 'I'll pass throughout', he spluttered as the TD announced that play was underway.

'Don't you dare call a spade a *shovel*', I warned him, 'and don't bid no-trumps first.'

Bridge began, and immediately on Board 1 Spouse, who was sitting South, broke Rule 1 by opening 'One Shovel'. I glared at him crossly, and he corrected to 'One Spade'.

I perused my hand and, when West passed, I made the practical bid of 4♠. East passed and Spouse broke Rule Two by bidding 4NT, Blackwood. I sighed inwardly, considered passing, but showed one Ace by responding 5◊. Spouse counted Aces carefully, found only one missing, and jumped to 6♠.

This had been the complete auction:

♠ Q 9 7 3
♡ 10 8 6
◊ 6 4
♣ A K Q 7

```
    N
W       E
    S
```

♠ A K 10 6 5
♡ 4
◊ A 9
♣ 10 9 4 3 2

South	West	North	East
Spouse		Wendy	
	NB	NB	NB
1♠	NB	4♠	NB
4NT	NB	5◊	NB
6♠	End		

I groaned inaudibly, but watched in amazement as Spouse ruffed the ♡K continuation after the initial ♡A lead, remembered to remove trumps, ruffed another heart, and discarded the losing diamond on the fifth club to bring home the contract. There was no stopping him now.

His confidence grew rapidly. By Board 12 he was advising me on bidding and play. By Board 24 he was giving opponents the benefit of his wisdom and bridge theories.

As we scored up at the end of the session, it emerged that on Board 1 – the 6♠ hand – PS had played in 4♡ as West:

Dealer: West
Game All

```
                                      ♠ Q 9 7 3
                                      ♡ 10 8 6
                                      ◊ 6 4
                                      ♣ A K Q 7
        ♠ 2                    ┌──────────┐      ♠ J 8 4
        ♡ A K 9 5 2            │    N     │      ♡ Q J 7 3
        ◊ Q 10 5 3 2        W  │          │  E   ◊ K J 8 7
        ♣ J 6                  │    S     │      ♣ 8 5
                              └──────────┘
                                      ♠ A K 10 6 5
                                      ♡ 4
                                      ◊ A 9
                                      ♣ 10 9 4 3 2
```

South	West	North	East
	PS		Millie
	1♡	NB	2♡
Dbl	NB	3♠	4♡
End			

North led the ♣A, followed by the ♣K. With the Aces of spades and diamonds still to lose, 4♡ minus one was an excellent score.

Other good scores followed, and our scratch team won the event by a narrow margin.

'When is the next event, then?' enquired Spouse enthusiastically.

I groaned. One bridge addict in a family is bad enough, but two…!

SOMETHING OF A RECORD

BY TONY SOWTER

Without any doubt, playing with Roman Smolski can be an exciting life. For example, consider your actions on this infamous hand from the 1993 Spring Foursomes, when you pick up the following collection with both sides vulnerable:

♠ J
♡ J 10 7 5 3
◇ J 10 6 5 2
♣ 8 4

Playing against one of England's strongest pairings, Gus Calderwood and Dick Shek, you hear your Left-Hand Opponent open 1♣, which in their methods shows a hand of at least 17 high-card points – nothing to do with clubs. Now you might think that when one of your opponents has advertised a very strong hand, the best thing to do is to sit back and let them get on with it. However, the modern approach is to get into the bidding as much as possible as, left to their own devices, the opponents are likely to bid the spots off the back of the cards. Accordingly, it came as no surprise to hear Smolski emerge with 1NT – no, not a strong hand, but systemically a weak two-suited hand with either clubs and hearts, or spades and diamonds. Next, you hear 2◇ on your right showing at least five diamonds and eight-plus points. What would you do now?

Well, it's fairly clear that if there are five diamonds on your right, your partner must have hearts and clubs – and with the opponents having at least game-going values, and an as yet undisclosed spade fit, it seems right to take out some more of their bidding space. Now 4♡ could prove to be marginally expensive, so I settled for a middle-of-the-road jump to 3♡.

Imagine my surprise when this was doubled, and partner ran to 3♠. Pass on the right, and it is again up to you.

Obviously, now partner is showing spades and diamonds, but with five diamonds on my right he can't actually have that many cards in the suit, and the known bad trump break gives one a certain feeling of foreboding. Anyway, for the moment there seems little harm in passing, for if 3♠ is passed out even six or seven down might not be too bad a result.

No such luck, for Calderwood duly doubles and this is passed back to you.

Well, it seems unlikely that 3♠ doubled is a good spot for your side, so obviously you are going to be forced to remove this to 4◊. However, it seemed to me that there might be some advantage to my partner playing the hand. First, the defence might be harder if his high cards were concealed and, perhaps more significantly, he deserved the pleasure of playing the hand having got us into this mess!

Of course, I could have bid 3NT, 4♣, or 4◊, but it seemed fairly safe to start with a redouble – after all, it was totally inconceivable that I could actually be expecting to make 3♠, so the redouble must be of the SOS variety, clearly for take-out.

Now, I have to be honest and say that at least I did achieve one of my objectives: partner played the hand – but in 3♠ redoubled! Apart from mounting a serious attack on the Guinness Book of Records, I can safely say that this was not a success. Witness the full hand:

West cashed the ♠A and switched to a club. East cashed all his trumps, and reverted to clubs. On the last club South was hopelessly squeezed: he could either discard the ◊A or unguard the ♡K.

As you might imagine, team-mates were not over-impressed. When they called out their

Dealer: East
Game All

	♠ J	
	♡ J 10 7 5 3	
	◊ J 10 6 5 2	
	♣ 8 4	
♠ A		♠ K Q 10 9 4 3
♡ 8 6	N	♡ A Q 9 2
◊ Q 9 7 4 3	W E	◊ –
♣ K J 9 7 5	S	♣ A Q 6
	♠ 8 7 6 5 2	
	♡ K 4	
	◊ A K 8	
	♣ 10 3 2	

score of plus 1370 for bidding and making 6♣, they were marginally surprised to find that they had lost 23 IMPs – and they were not pleased to be told that if they had managed to bid and make their lay-down grand slam in spades, they could have held the loss to just 21 IMPs!

Now you may not think much of my partner's initial choice of action, but I suppose that A–K–x is not far off being a four-card suit – and frankly, if I had simply converted 3♠ to 4◊, then the resultant penalty might well have been only 1100 points, and we would have gained 7 IMPs on the board.

I bet that not many of you have lost a bigger penalty than 5200!

DOUBLE GAME SWING

BY SU BURN

What is the greatest number of points that you have seen turn on the play of a single card to the first trick? On this deal from this year's National Pairs, the swing was 2050 aggregate points!

I was North and my partner, Isobel Belcher, was South. West opened with a weak 1NT, and I decided to overcall 2♡ on the North hand. I had once heard Roman Smolski describe one of his partner's bids as 'likely to be based more on distribution than high cards', and I had that fine phrase ready for when partner asked me afterwards what on earth I thought I was doing.

```
Dealer: West    ♠ 6 2
E/W Vul         ♡ Q J 10 9 8 5 3
                ◇ –
                ♣ 10 9 7 6
♠ A J 8 4                       ♠ Q 10 7 5
♡ 7 4            ┌─────────┐     ♡ K 2
◇ K Q 10 8      │    N    │     ◇ A 9 6 4 3
♣ K 5 2         │ W     E │     ♣ Q 8
                │    S    │
                └─────────┘
                ♠ K 9 3
                ♡ A 6
                ◇ J 7 5 2
                ♣ A J 4 3
```

East bid a natural 2NT and, not for the first time in our partnership, South wondered why she seemed to be playing with a fifty-point pack. Eventually, she settled for a raise to 3♡. What do you think West might bid now – if he should bid at all, that is?

Having already denied a five-card spade suit by his 1NT opening, West might have steered his partnership into their best game-contract with a bid of 3♠, which East would happily have raised to 4♠. As it was, he decided to bid 3NT. Had I known that our side could actually make 4♡, I would now have bid it, but I naïvely thought that I had done enough bidding already. When 3NT was passed round to Isobel, she doubled it – as who would not? I was not terribly happy with this development, but there seemed little to do but pass and lead the ♡Q.

An awful lot of match points swung on what West played from dummy at trick one. Had he played low, he would have made at least ten tricks for a score of 950 to East–West. As it was, he went up with the ♡K and had to exercise considerable patience before gaining the lead. When the smoke cleared, the contract was four down doubled for 1100 to North–South!

BRIDGE ON THE INSIDE

BY COLIN PORCH

The essence of a good con', enthused Sykes in his just-stick-with-me-I-know-what-I'm-talking-about voice, 'is to let your victim think that he is the one doing the conning.'

'Any particular victim in mind?' enquired Tiny, not really wishing to know; his interest was vested primarily in the bar of fruit-and-nut lying on the table. If only he could divert Sykes's attention for just a second… As if reading his thoughts, Sykes casually picked up the chocolate and placed it carefully in his pocket.

'Who do you think?' retorted Sykes. 'That blasted Legal Eagle from C Wing. Who else?'

Tiny grimaced. He privately doubted anybody's ability to con *that* gentleman and, as Sykes's partner, he tended to suffer as each successive attempt went wrong. Still, he was prepared to listen…

'Take this hand', invited Sykes, pulling a dirty piece of paper from his pocket. 'Many years ago, a Duke or something lost a wager of £20,000 when he claimed that thirteen tricks could not be made if clubs were trumps. And', he added conspiratorially, 'it was also good enough for James Bond!' *

```
                    ♠ 10 9 8 7
                    ♡ 6 5 4 3
                    ◇ –
                    ♣ 7 6 5 3 2
  ♠ 6 5 4 3 2     ┌─────────┐     ♠ A K Q J
  ♡ 10 9 8 7 2    │    N    │     ♡ A K Q J
  ◇ J 10 9        │ W     E │     ◇ A K
  ♣ –             │    S    │     ♣ K J 9
                  └─────────┘
                    ♠ –
                    ♡ –
                    ◇ Q 8 7 6 5 4 3 2
                    ♣ A Q 10 8 4
```

Tiny perked up. He was not capable of reading the books, but he adored James Bond films; no further recommendation was needed. He

* In *Moonraker* by Ian Fleming – hands rotated for convenience.

hardly listened as Sykes explained how the diamonds were established with two ruffs in dummy, finessing against East's clubs on the way back. His voice dropped two octaves as he mentally took the place of his super-hero.

'What's my mission?' he asked.

Sykes sat back contentedly. His trap was set, Tiny having successfully substituted the prepared deck when cutting the cards. The stakes had been raised to five roll-ups per hundred, and his mind wandered blissfully into the realms of mental arithmetic as he contemplated his profit on the evening.

East, whose name Sykes could never remember, opened 4NT, asking partner to show an Ace. West responded 5♣, not having any, and 5NT from East was intended to end the auction. Now a 6◇ bid from Sykes was a bit risky – but what East could resist a double on that hand? After the double, Sykes could bid 7♣, giving the auction an air, at least, of authenticity. East's double seemed automatic, and Sykes left it to Tiny to redouble, as planned.

But now what? West, the Legal Eagle, was sitting back in his chair, clearly contemplating some action. Surely he was out of the auction? If he was, he certainly showed no sign of recognizing the fact. Eventually he placed his cards carefully on the table and bid 7♠ in his low, precise voice. Tiny doubled, to Sykes' dismay (East could not make 7♠, but could West?), two passes followed – then a resounding 'Redouble!'.

Did Sykes detect a note of triumph in the voice?

Using hearts as entries, and apparently oblivious to the waves of hatred emanating from his right, the Legal Eagle found no difficulty in ruffing dummy's clubs in hand, leaving dummy high.

Five minutes later found Sykes and Tiny, still thunderstruck from the ordeal, wandering back along the landing. As they passed the Legal Eagle's cell, they could plainly hear his voice as it wafted out onto the wing.

'The essence of a good con...', he was saying...

97

POLISH PUZZLE

BY NIGEL GUTHRIE

West is to make 7NT against any distribution and defence:

♠ A K Q J	**N**	♠ 10
♡ A 8		♡ K J 10 9
◊ A 8 7	**W** **E**	◊ K Q 10 9
♣ A 8 7 6	**S**	♣ K Q 10 9

Krysztos Martens published a 'sure-trick' teaser, like this one, in *Przeglad Brydzowy*, the Polish bridge magazine. This pretty problem has perplexed plenty of players. Stuart Maurice, to whom I am indebted, showed it to me. Suffice to say that I stumbled on the surprisingly simple solution after only a fortnight of frustration.

Solution on page 214.

DISCARDING METHODS

I was playing at our local club in a difficult 3NT contract where I could see only eight tricks. I deliberated for ages, then played a third round of diamonds on which RHO discarded.

I asked his partner what discards they were playing, and quick as a flash she replied: 'That one was out of boredom!'

Ann McBride

THE ART OF DECEPTION

BY BRIAN SENIOR

Were you brought up to believe that honesty is always the best policy? Perhaps in everyday life this is true, though fewer people seem to adhere to such standards than once was the case. What is quite certain is that, at the bridge table, adding a little deceit to your make-up whether in bidding, play, or defence, will make you a far tougher opponent than if you always have your bid, always play the technically correct card, and always signal honestly.

When I talk about deceit, I am suggesting that you should try to mislead your opponents by the *order* in which you play your cards, not the *manner* in which you play them. If, for example, declarer leads up towards dummy's K–J–x and you hesitate with Q–x–x in the hope that he will place you with the Ace and mis-guess, you are not being deceptive, you are quite simply a cheat.

As declarer, you can let your imagination run riot and false-card to your heart's content – the point being, of course, that you have no partner to worry about, so only your opponents can be misled. It is important, however, always to play a plausible false-card if you are to succeed in your deception. For example, you play in 4♥ after South has overcalled 1♠, and North leads the ♠2:

♠ Q J 10

N
W   E
S

♠ K 6 3

You play dummy's ♠3 and South wins with the ♠A. The only card which gives you a chance is the Jack. Think about it for a moment: would North lead the 2 from Q–J–2 or J–10–2? No, but he might from Q–10–2.

In defence, you need to be more careful as you now have a partner to consider. Take the following two situations:

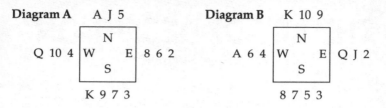

Diagram A A J 5

N
Q 10 4 W   E 8 6 2
S

K 9 7 3

Diagram B K 10 9

N
A 6 4 W   E Q J 2
S

8 7 5 3

In (A) you are West. Declarer (South) leads to the Jack, cashes the Ace, and leads a third round. If your remaining card is the Queen, he is bound to drop it, because you were known to hold it when the Jack scored. If your last card is the Ten, however, declarer has a guess. This is an obligatory false-card, and cannot harm partner.

In (B) you are East. Declarer leads low to the 9. If you win with the Jack, his next play is likely to be low to the Ten, isn't it? Suppose, however, that you win the first trick with the Queen. On the second round your partner may either hesitate – thereby giving the game away – or even take his Ace seeing no point in ducking. Your 'clever' play served to create a problem for partner, not for declarer. Perhaps 'clever' is not the right adjective to use.

Let me finish with a complete deal. It comes from the 1993 European Pairs Championship (consolation event, alas).

Dealer: East
E/W Vul

♠ 5 3 2
♡ A 8 4
◇ A 5
♣ K 10 9 7 2

♠ A Q J 8 7
♡ J 6
◇ K Q 9 8 7
♣ 6

N
W   E
S

♠ 10 6 4
♡ 10 9 7 5 3
◇ 10 3
♣ J 8 5

♠ K 9
♡ K Q 2
◇ J 6 4 2
♣ A Q 4 3

South	West	North	East
	Senior		Price
			NB
1◇	1♠	2♣	NB
2NT (a)	NB	3NT	End

(a) 15+ Points, game-forcing.

Expecting partner to have little or nothing, and not wanting to give a trick away, I started with a safe ♡J. Declarer won with his King and ran the clubs. I threw the ♢8, ♠8, ♠7, and ♠Q, while declarer pitched a diamond and partner the ♡10 and ♠4. Next, declarer cashed the Ace and Queen of hearts and I pitched the ♢7, trying to look as though I was 6–2–4–1. Declarer now played a diamond to the Ace, and I confirmed this impression by playing the Queen.

Finally, declarer played a second diamond and ducked when David Price played the Ten. Had I actually been 6–2–4–1, I would have had to win the King (establishing his Jack) and I would then have had to lead a spade up to his King for eleven tricks. In reality, however, I was able to underplay the ♢9, and partner's spade switch held declarer to nine tricks.

Minus 400 looks like a huge result, but it was actually only a 69% score (as opposed to 30% for minus 430), as many Wests had come in over a strong no-trump and played in 2♠ doubled for plus 670 or minus 200.

If you can foresee the possible ending, there are many opportunities, as here, to play on declarer's greed when playing match-pointed pairs.

A USEFUL RULE

Wife, opening the bidding out of turn, and finding that her husband has to pass throughout the auction: 'That's a relief, I've been trying to get him to shut up all afternoon!'

(from the Surrey CBA Bulletin)

THE BEST ROUTE?

BY DAVID PERKINS

Arriving at the correct destination is of critical importance, but the route you take can have an effect on the result. In a recent teams-of-four match, the biggest swing occurred on the following board, although both declarers were in the same contract:

```
Dealer: North   ♠ J 9
Game All        ♡ Q J 10 8 7 2
                ◇ A 6
                ♣ 9 5 4

♠ 5                          ♠ Q 10 7 6 4 2
♡ A 6 5 4          N         ♡ 3
◇ K J 10 9 7   W       E     ◇ 8 3
♣ A J 3            S         ♣ Q 8 7 2

                ♠ A K 8 3
                ♡ K 9
                ◇ Q 5 4 2
                ♣ K 10 6
```

At one table, North passed and South opened 1NT(15–17). West passed and North went into a huddle. 'Why on earth won't my partner play transfers?', he thought. 'I would bid 2◇ and raise his 2♡ to 4♡.' After some further agonizing, he bid 3NT. West led the ◇J and now it was South's turn to worry. If the ◇K was on his right, he was going to have to find an entry to dummy from ♠J–9. However, when he played small, the ◇K did not appear, so he was able to establish the hearts and enter dummy with the ◇A. When East discarded too many spades, South ended up with eleven tricks.

'I could have beaten the contract, if I had led the ◇K,' said West. 'Difficult to find', retorted South, 'but you might have tried it in the hope of finding the ◇Q singleton in dummy.' No-one at the table saw much chance of West finding such a killing lead in the other room.

But events there had taken a different turn. North opened a weak 2♡ and, when South ended up as declarer in 3NT, West had a further reason for leading the ◇K. From his own heart holding he could see the need to attack an outside entry to dummy, and that entry might be the ◇A. So the ◇K was led, and declarer ended up with only six tricks.

Both sides applauded West's brilliant lead. West modestly claimed that the ◇K was 'pretty automatic' on the bidding! And – for obvious reasons – the first South is still unwilling to play transfers over 1NT!

THERE'S NOWT SO QUEER AS FOLK

BY JOHN BEARD

I have been running successful bridge courses and holidays for twenty-five years. In that time, I have been fortunate enough to have had wonderful groups of people to deal with, and many funny things have happened. Let me share a few.

Fifteen Rounds

My wife, Angela, and I were running a bridge course for some sixty people, and after the duplicate session on the Saturday evening twenty people settled down to play cut-in rubber bridge. It seemed as though almost everybody felt peckish, so we ordered fifteen rounds of sandwiches plus coffee. After about forty minutes nothing had arrived, so we chased our order and finally we were served. We played until about 1.30 a.m., then decided to call it a night.

When Angela and I went back to our room, we found out why the sandwiches had taken so long. They were on every surface – all fifteen rounds of them!

The Bean System

There was a gentleman who played with lots of different partners. On one occasion, he sat down and his new partner told him that he played Acol.

'Ah!' commented the gentleman. 'The Beans System.'

'Beans?' asked his partner.

'Yes: there are fifty-seven different varieties!'

Marital Bridge

Two husbands were talking together about their wives. One was heard saying, 'She always thought I was quite bright until we started playing bridge!'

Alerting Procedure

A husband and wife partnership were playing in a duplicate session. The wife, South, made a conventional bid and knocked on the table.

'You can't alert your own bids!' expostulated West.

'But my husband always expects me to do everything for him', was the apologetic reply.

103

REVERSES UNRAVELLED

BY DAVID PARRY

One of the most confusing areas of basic bidding theory is the so-called reverse. Part of the reason is undoubtedly that the very name is a misnomer. Take the following two simple sequences, for example:

Auction 1		**Auction 2**	
Opener	*Responder*	*Opener*	*Responder*
1♡	1♠	1♢	1♠
2♢		2♡	

In both sequences opener has shown length in hearts and diamonds, and normally responder will choose one of these suits as trumps. If responder is weak, of course, he will want to stop at the lowest available level, and this is where the difficulty occurs.

In **Auction 1** responder can stop in either 2♢ (by passing) or 2♡. In **Auction 2**, he can still stop in 2♡ by passing (although, in practice, most pairs treat this bid as forcing – see Partnership Understandings below), but must go to 3♢ if this is the suit he prefers. Clearly extra strength (points) will be needed to make the extra tricks, and since responder may have no more than six points the onus is on opener to have a stronger hand to follow the path in **Auction 2**.

Definition

If opener bids two suits in such an order that responder will have to go to the three level to give preference to opener's first suit, then the opener is said to have reversed.

Strength

A reverse requires a minimum of 16 points; a non-reverse may be made on any hand (12+ points).

Consequences

The most important point to note is that if you do not have 16 points, you cannot reverse. For instance, suppose you hold the hands shown right.

On *Hand A* you open 1♡ and if partner responds 1♠ you can happily give partner a choice of trump suits by rebidding 2♢ – which is not a reverse.

Hand A	*Hand B*
♠ 8 7	♠ 8 7
♡ A Q 6 5 4	♡ A Q 6 5
♢ A K 6 5	♢ A K 6 5 4
♣ 5 4	♣ 5 4

On *Hand B* you start with 1◇, but now, if partner responds 1♠, you have a problem. To give partner a choice of trump suits (always best, if possible) would entail rebidding 2♡. This would be a reverse, and would therefore require 16 points. Obviously you are not strong enough, so you have to simply rebid 2◇.

Other consequences are:

1. Opener guarantees a minimum of five cards in his first suit.
2. If opener reverses at the two level, then his first suit will definitely be longer than his second, but if he reverses at the three level then all that can be said with certainty is that his first suit will be at least as long as his second, and will contain at least five cards.

Notes

1. Although you must have 16 points to reverse, it does not follow that you must reverse just because you have 16 points. Always bid your suits in the normal order – longest first or higher-ranking of two equals.
2. A rebid by opener at the one level can never be a reverse.
3. A reverse at the two level (1◇ – 1♠ – 2♡) is sometimes called a *low reverse*, and a reverse at the three level (1♡ – 2◇ – 3♣) is sometimes called a *high reverse*.

Partnership Understandings

In the modern style, at least the following agreements would be considered standard:

1. A non-reverse by opener is not forcing.
2. A reverse by opener after a one-level response is forcing for one round.
3. A reverse by opener after a two-level response is game-forcing.

Simple Rule

If you struggle with the concept of reverses, the following rule of thumb may help:

- After an opening of one of a suit, two of that suit is defined as the *barrier*.
- A rebid in a new suit below the barrier is not a reverse. A rebid in a new suit above the barrier is a reverse.

For example, consider the two auctions at the beginning of this article:

In **Auction 1**, 1♡ is the opening; 2♡ is the barrier; 2◇ is below the barrier; 2◇ is not a reverse.

In **Auction 2**, 1◇ is the opening; 2◇ is the barrier; 2♡ is above the barrier; 2♡ is a reverse.

CROSSWORD PUZZLE

BY ROGER TROWELL

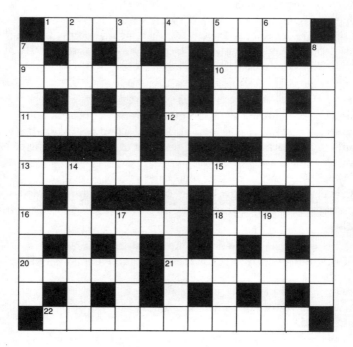

ACROSS:

1 Grisly charm, shown a lot by experts? (4, 2, 5)

9 Less straight and more wrong. (7)

10 Invigorate Wren with energy head to tail. (5)

11 Top expert backs into junction – the nut! (5)

12 Kerfuffle broken into after return of dog. (7)

13 Always like feeling thrills after several spills. (13)

16 10 and 1 together make one of these. (7)

18 What you like to get from partner or boss. (5)

20 Swish affair, but conducted in the hay? (5)

21 Diamonds with what 8 is, is cool. (3-4)

22 African bird, following suit, coins coin. (5, 6)

DOWN:

2 Like an eye to the ear – that's Nahuatl! (5)
3 Laid back about pot only once per diem. (7)
4 What blazers, presumably, are not! (4-9)
5 Tenor in full voice like the one, the only – Richard Tauber! (5)
6 Leading player did this in ruffing finesse. (7)
7 Lather-upper makes speed. (6, 5)
8 I amount to two 16s plus 5 (beware!). (6-5)
14 Sounds like I panic on the bridle. (3-4)
15 Truth-teller says he's from the Middle East – i.e. liar's wrong! (7)
17 Take a sedative – get relaxed therefrom. (5)
19 Get used to ruin crashing on east's head. (5)

Solution on page 214.

THE JOYS OF BRIDGE

BY RUTH EDMONDSON

Last Thursday I set off to play in a Simultaneous Pairs event at my nearest bridge club. The evening started well – I found a parking space! We had some luck on the first two rounds, and were set for an enjoyable evening.

On the third round, there was a problem at the Director's table and I was asked to give a ruling. A quick phone call to our local EBU Director, and I confidently gave a ruling – only to have two of the players disagree with me. Tempers became somewhat frayed; an appeal was lodged, and I intended to organize three players to hear the appeal at the end of the evening, when something happened to put it right out of my mind.

The police knocked on the door to say that there had been some fighting at the top of the road and several cars were damaged. I smiled smugly, as my car was parked at the other end of the road. However, a friend said that his car too was there – and damaged – so I dashed out to find a windscreen-wiper beyond repair and a policeman looking at a whole row of similarly damaged cars. I must add here that I was very lucky, as some people had had their doors and wings kicked in.

The only hand I can remember from the evening is Board 33, which was not part of the Simultaneous Pairs. I was West and picked up the hand below:

♠ 6
♡ 10 8 7 5
♢ A 10 6 4 2
♣ 7 5 3

My partner opened the bidding with 2♣ (showing eight playing-tricks in an unspecified suit). I was looking round the room, wondering whom I could ask to sit on the Appeals Committee, and promptly passed! The next hand rescued me – thinking I had a bad hand, he entered the bidding with a 2♠ bid. The complete auction was:

South	West	North	East
			2♣ (a)
NB	NB	2♠	3♡
3♠	4♡	4♠	5♡
5♠	6♡	End	

(a) Benjaminised Acol, see above.

This contract made without any trouble, leaving North (whose car also had been vandalized) slightly embarrassed – and probably wondering whether there are any joys to be derived from bridge!

PLAN YOUR DEFENCE

BY BOB ROWLANDS

Dealer: East
Game All

♠ J
♡ A Q 9 6 2
◊ 10 9 7
♣ Q J 5 2

South	West	North	East
			1♣
1♡	Dbl (a)	4♡	End

(a) Sputnik, showing four spades.

♠ 10 5 3 2
♡ 10 4
◊ A J 5 4 3
♣ K 4

```
      N
W          E
      S
```

Against 4♡ by South you, West, lead the ♣K to ♣2, ♣3, and ♣6. How do you continue?

Solution on page 215.

FASCINATING MYSTERIES

Did you know that the most common bidding sequence in English bridge is 'One banana – Two oranges – Three grapes?'

This is shorthand in high-level post-mortems for 'One of (any) suit – Two of (any other) suit', etc.

Serious players would be shocked at a sequence that went 'One potato – Two peas – Three cauliflowers'. Why only some fruits, and no vegetable, should enjoy such popularity in bridge is one of the game's fascinating mysteries.

JUMPS IN THE LAKE

BY JASON HACKETT

Every two years trials are held for British pairs under the age of twenty-five, the aim being to form and train a squad from which a team capable of finishing in the top three in the European Junior Championships, and thereby qualifying for the World Junior Championships, is selected. Between the trials and the EJC the squad participates in a number of activities, some of which have nothing to do with bridge!

Approximately every second month, the squad meets for a training weekend. Six Under-25 pairs and six Under-21 pairs meet on Saturday morning (usually in London, at the London School of Bridge, where rooms are generously provided free of charge) and listen to a seminar taken by expert tutors such as Brian Senior, Andrew Robson, and David Burn. A 48-board match is played against a team of internationals, and we also participate in useful exercises such as filling in ques-

tionnaires about defensive methods and seeing how few answers correspond to those given by partner.

In the months between, the British Bridge League sends a team to play in various matches. These range from matches against county teams to friendly matches against continental junior teams, and from the Channel Trophy to the EC Championships, all leading up to the big event – the European Junior Championships. Usually, all squad members are given at least one match; however, players in contention for the EC and European Championship Junior Teams play in most of the matches, and it was in one of the friendly matches that I played one of my best-ever hands:

```
Dealer: East                                  ♠ Q 9
Game All                                      ♡ Q J 3
                                              ◇ J 10 9 8 6
                                              ♣ 7 5 2

                       ♠ J 10 4        ┌─────────────┐      ♠ K 6 3 2
                       ♡ K 8 5         │      N      │      ♡ 10 7 4 2
                       ◇ 7 3           │ W        E  │      ◇ K Q 5
                       ♣ K 10 9 6 4    │      S      │      ♣ 8 3
                                       └─────────────┘

                                              ♠ A 8 7 5
  South     West     North     East           ♡ A 9 6
  Jason     Justin                            ◇ A 4 2
  Hackett   Hackett                           ♣ A Q J
                              NB
  2NT (a)   NB       3NT      End
```

(a) 19–21 points.

West led the ♣9, which came round to my Jack. I then played a heart to the Queen, and ran the ◇J. The ◇10 was led next, covered by the Queen and taken with my Ace. I now played a spade to West's Jack, ducking in dummy.

At this point West played the ♠10, covered by the Queen and King, and taken with my Ace, so I ended up by scoring the ♠A–8–7, two heart tricks, two diamond tricks, and two club tricks. However, even if East does not cover the ♠Q, or if West returns a low spade, I can still make the contract by eliminating the spades and throwing in West with the ♡K to lead into my club tenace.

This hand helped us to a 3-IMP win in a friendly match against Israel at the 1991 Easter *Guardian*.

After a year, the U-25 squad is trimmed down to four pairs, a team squad. Currently these are Danny Davies (21) from Sheffield, who works in insurance; Philip Souter (23), an Oxford student; Justin Hackett (22), a student in Preston; Jeff Allerton (23), an accountant from Manchester; Tom Townsend, (21) a Cambridge student; Peter Dunsby (23), an accountant in Crawley; David Bakhshi (18), a promising young player who is about to study in Manchester; finally, myself (22), a Manchester-based bridge player.

In addition to the usual squad activities, we use a sports psychologist who assists the team in avoiding friction between players, and addresses the problem of keeping up team spirit – quite important if you have to play for ten to fourteen days. To this end, during our last weekend meeting we all spent time on an assault course, bivouacking, and performing acrobatics in canoes!

The value of this was shown at the last EC Championships, where team spirit stayed high despite an awful start. A change in partnerships produced fourteen wins from fifteen matches, and in the end we missed the bronze medal by a tantalizing 1 VP.

This board would have helped. South is dealer at Game All. What would you lead with the hand below?

	♠ K 9 8 6 4	South	West	North	East
	♡ 10 5 3		*Justin*		*Jason*
	◊ 7 4	2♡ (a)	NB	2♠ (b)	NB
	♣ Q J 3	3◊	Dbl (c)	3NT	4♠
		NB	NB	Dbl	NB
		4NT	Dbl	NB	NB
		Redbl	End		

(a) Weak Two in spades, or Acol Two in a minor.
(b) To play opposite a weak two.
(c) Take-out.

This board came up on the last round against the Netherlands, who had a team rule that any player going for minus 1400 had to jump into the lake outside the playing area.

A diamond lead nets plus 400. My spade lead costs you minus 1120, an horrendous swing of 37 IMPs (minus 16 instead of plus 21), and 7 VPs. A club or diamond lead, and North would have been awarded *two* jumps into the lake!

JUSTICE AT BRIDGE

BY RON PICK

Aggression sometimes pays, but the rewards should be earned. Consider my problems as South on this hand, where I was declarer in 7NT (well, it was pairs).

West leads the ◊9 and one looks at the top twelve tricks! The first thought is, obviously, 'Which finesse shall we take?'

However, having read up to page 3 of our book on squeezes, we know all about automatic squeezes and Vienna Coups. A squeeze will work if either opponent holds both black Kings – and we still have a finesse in reserve. We cash the ♣A, and run off our red-suit winners to arrive at:

```
Dealer: South      ♠ J 7 5 4
E/W Vul            ♡ 10 7
                   ◊ K Q J 10 8
                   ♣ A J

♠ K 3          N          ♠ 10 9 8 6
♡ 9 2                     ♡ 8 6 5 3
◊ 9 4      W       E      ◊ 6 5 3 2
♣ K 9 8 7 5 4 3    S      ♣ 10

                   ♠ A Q 2
                   ♡ A K Q J 4
                   ◊ A 7
                   ♣ Q 6 2
```

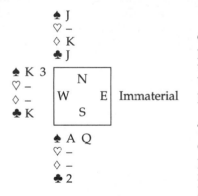

```
        ♠ J
        ♡ –
        ◊ K
        ♣ J
♠ K 3        N
♡ –                     Immaterial
◊ –      W       E
♣ K          S
        ♠ A Q
        ♡ –
        ◊ –
        ♣ 2
```

At this point I lead dummy's last diamond, part with my ♣2, and watch West squirm. Whichever card he throws, I've made my contract.

Sadly, this is fairy tale. The actual hand was not quite like the one above. I played it exactly in this manner, but unfortunately the club layout was rather different. It was a pity that I had not read page 4 of the squeeze manual, because then I could (perhaps) have coped with the actual hand, which was:

```
            ♠ J 7 5 4
            ♡ 10 7
            ◇ K Q J 10 8
            ♣ A 4
♠ K 3        ┌─────────┐   ♠ 10 9 8 6
♡ 9 8 5 2    │    N    │   ♡ 6 3
◇ 9 4        │ W     E │   ◇ 6 5 3 2
♣ K J 10 9 8 │    S    │   ♣ 7 5 3
             └─────────┘
            ♠ A Q 2
            ♡ A K Q J 4
            ◇ A 7
            ♣ Q 6 2
```

If West plays a club, I throw a spade, then I play a club to the Ace to drop the now singleton King, and a club back to my hand to make the last two tricks with ♣Q and ♠A. If West discards a spade, I throw a club, cash my ♠A, cross to dummy with the ♣A, and score my thirteenth trick with the ♠J.

I should have played the hand straight out, cashing the ten red tricks. This results in the four-card ending below, in which I am just about to lead the last heart from my hand, and West must bare one of his black Kings:

```
            ♠ J 7
            ♡ –
            ◇ –
            ♣ A 4
♠ K 3        ┌─────────┐
♡ –          │    N    │
◇ –          │ W     E │  Immaterial
♣ K J        │    S    │
             └─────────┘
            ♠ A
            ♡ A
            ◇ –
            ♣ Q 2
```

So the sad truth is that I did go one down. I really must work harder at my technique, and try to master not just simple squeezes but also the *criss-cross* variety outlined above. Who knows, I may come across a hand like that once again in the next thirty years.

VALUE YOUR PART-SCORES

BY HAROLD SCHOGGER

Many players are of the opinion that unless all hands are bid to game, or higher, you cannot do well at duplicate pairs. Nothing is further from the truth, and I think this is just a feeble excuse for overbidding.

Experts gain more match-points on part-score hands than they do on the more glamorous slam hands, and many more hands are played in the part-score zone. In future think about passing, once your partner has made a limit-response, and you will be pleasantly surprised that your two-level contract wins all the match points. Perhaps the opponents will protect and push you higher – but why go higher if they do not push you!

```
Dealer: South                          ♠ 6 5 2
Love All                               ♡ 10 9 6
                                       ◊ Q J 10 8 7
                                       ♣ K J
                    ♠ K J 7                          ♠ 10 3
                    ♡ Q 7 2       N                  ♡ K 5 3
                    ◊ K 6 3    W     E               ◊ 9 5 4 2
                    ♣ 10 9 5 4       S               ♣ A Q 7 2

                                       ♠ A Q 9 8 4
South   West   North   East            ♡ A J 8 4
1♠      NB     1NT     NB              ◊ A
2♡      NB     2♠      End             ♣ 8 6 3
```

On this hand, many pairs were playing in 3♠ and some Souths reached the dizzy heights of 4♠ and 4♡ – receiving well-deserved bottoms for their incompetent efforts. Simple bidding as suggested above allows North to give preference to South's first suit, and South should be happy to play at the two level for an above-average match-point score of minus 50 against all the overbidders who conceded minus 100, or minus 150.

For South to make any move forward is wishful thinking, in view of North's original 1NT bid. North must have so many good cards, and the distribution of the opponents' cards must be very friendly, for a game contract to make.

WHEN IT LOOKS EASY...

BY PETER ROWLETT

I only ever partnered Geoff Walshaw once. Geoff was a seasoned
County player, a founder-member both of Kettering Bridge Club and
the County Association. He also was a gifted raconteur with a fund of
bridge stories that he could draw on whenever occasion demanded.

I was a relative newcomer to the game, and all I had to recommend
me was enthusiasm. So I was both delighted and surprised when Geoff
asked me if I would partner him one evening. It was just an ordinary
club duplicate session, and I tried hard not to make mistakes; but it was
his experience and skill that brought us in to second place. I remember
a remark he made: 'When it looks easy, pause and think.'

We arranged to play again; but Geoff was seriously ill at this time,
and had to go into hospital. He died soon afterwards. However, a year
or two beforehand he had created a new County competition, a knock-
out rubber-bridge contest designed to bring club and casual players
together. It was to be bridge for fun – which Geoff thought was the
point of bridge.

The Geoff Walshaw Rubber Bridge Knock-out Competition is still
going strong, and for the past five or six years I've had the pleasure of
organizing it for Northamptonshire. Successive years have seen increasing numbers of participants, and in 1992–93 sixty-four pairs from all
over the county signed up. We've even introduced the Walshaw Plate,
for pairs knocked out in the first round of the main event.

As well as organizing the competition, I take part in it too: some time
ago my partner and I won the trophy, a victory mitigated by the fact
that only seventeen pairs entered that year. Last year, though, in a
much larger field, we reached the final and lost the 30-hand match on
the last deal.

That was bad luck. This year we were knocked out in the second round
– again, on the final hand when we were ahead. This time I think it was
due to mulishness on my part. I played in blinkers. Judge for yourselves.

When Hand 30 was dealt, our opponents needed game and rubber
to beat us. Anything less, and the match was ours. This was the deal:

116

```
              ♠ A Q 5 4
              ♡ –
              ◇ 10 4 3
              ♣ A J 9 5 4 2
  ♠ J 9 2         ┌─────────┐        ♠ K 8 3
  ♡ 10 8 4        │    N    │        ♡ K Q J 7 5
  ◇ A 9 7 5    W  │         │  E     ◇ K J 6
  ♣ 8 7 3         │    S    │        ♣ Q 10
                  └─────────┘
              ♠ 10 7 6
              ♡ A 9 6 3 2
              ◇ Q 8 2
              ♣ K 6
```

North dealt and opened 1♣. Sitting East, I breathed a sigh of relief: game North–South did not look likely with a good defensive hand like mine. Rather than double, I made a jump overcall of 2♡. South thought for a while, then bid 2NT. My partner West ventured to 3♡. North passed, as did I. South sat for a while, presumably doing calculations – would 3♡ doubled be enough to give them the match? However, her partner was almost certainly marked with a void in hearts, and South might find herself making only the Ace. In the end, she bid 3NT. I didn't bother to double. The match was ours.

Partner led the ♡8 on which I played the Jack. South won with the Ace, then played the ♣K. When we both followed, she paused for a long time, deciding whether to play to drop the Queen or take the finesse.

If she had decided to go for the drop, which succeeds, we would have won the match. She would then be locked in dummy and be limited to eight tricks – one heart, six clubs, and the ♠A. Neither I nor my partner would have been uncomfortably squeezed; and at some stage he would have been able to indicate his diamond holding, allowing me to lead happily away from my diamond tenace.

However, declarer decided to play by the book, and tried the finesse. Winning with the ♣Q, I played the ♡K–Q. Partner followed with the ♡10 and ♡4 respectively; and in an unblinkered state I would have worked out that he had only three of the suit. What had he got to justify his raise to 3♡? Since I could now place virtually everything except the ◇A, it was reasonable to suppose he was holding it. But I wasn't reasoning. Irrationally reluctant to underlead my ◇K, and confident that our opponents couldn't make the contract, I threw down the ♡7...('When it looks easy, pause and think!')

With a little murmur of satisfaction, declarer accepted the gift of two more heart tricks. It was what she needed to wrap up nine tricks for game, rubber, and match.

'My fault', said my partner, Rod. 'I should have started with the ♡10.'
Partners like this are hard to find, and should be cherished.

117

A SMALL MISTAKE

BY JACK KROES

The first EC University Teams Championships were organized this year in Antwerp. Eleven of the twelve EC countries sent a team to compete in this new event.

In the two semi-finals, which followed an initial round robin, Germany beat Israel 45–37, and Great Britain defeated Denmark 78–41. In the final Germany won 79–74.

The British team played well throughout, and it seemed unfair that a small mistake in the round-robin match against France should cost so dearly:

Dealer: West
Game All

```
                              ♠ Q 10 8 6 4
                              ♡ J 3
                              ◊ K 7 4
                              ♣ K 7 5
        ♠ K J 7        ┌──────────┐     ♠ A 5 3
        ♡ K Q 8        │    N     │     ♡ 9 6 2
        ◊ A Q 3        │  W   E   │     ◊ J 10 6 2
        ♣ A J 4 2      │    S     │     ♣ 8 6 3
                       └──────────┘
                              ♠ 9 2
                              ♡ A 10 7 5 4
                              ◊ 9 8 5
                              ♣ Q 10 9
```

South	West	North	East
	Mauberquez		Oursel
	2NT	NB	3♣ (a)
NB	3NT	End	

(a) Baron, asking for 4-card suits.

After winning the opening lead of the ♣6 with his ♣J, declarer played the ◊Q which held the trick. He continued with ◊A and a small diamond, taken by North with the ◊K. A spade to the Ace followed, then declarer cashed dummy's ◊J, on which South, West, and North pitched respectively the ♡4, the ♣2, and the ♣5.

This last card proved to be a very costly mistake, for now the ♡2 was led to the ♡K and then declarer led the ♣4, which ran to South's ♣9. South had nothing better to return than another club. West rose with the Ace and crushed North's King!

After cashing his ♠K, declarer exited with a club to South's ♣Q. All South could do was cash his ♡A, and reluctantly concede the last trick to declarer's ♡Q – thus enabling West to make his contract.

THE STRONG PAUSE

BY CHRIS KINLOCH

NO MATTER WHERE YOU ARE, IT IS USUALLY POSSIBLE TO FIND A GAME IN PROGRESS

One advantage of playing bridge is that no matter where you are, it is usually possible to find a game in progress. And so it is in Hong Kong – as I found out during a business-cum-holiday trip.

The main system used is Strong No-trump, Weak Twos in diamonds, hearts, and spades, Five-card majors, and either a Better Minor or a One Club Opening with a minimum of two cards. A few pairs play Precision, and some expatriates play Acol.

The standard varies from club to club. The best players are very good (Hong Kong played in the last Bermuda Bowl final), but the level of expertise falls off quickly.

Fortunately for the visitor, clubs play on different evenings, which means that an aficionado can play every evening of the week.

Bridge at the Hong Kong Cricket Club is very relaxed, with ample time being given by the Director for the purchase of very cheap – but most palatable – food and drink. Play starts at 8.00 p.m., with the result that not many boards are played – normally eighteen or twenty.

Playing with a totally strange partner, I picked up the following hand as South:

♠ K 10 9 6 5
♡ 6
◇ K 4 3
♣ A 9 7 4

This was the bidding:

South	West	North	East
		NB	NB
NB	1◇ (a)	Dbl	1♡
1♠ (b)	2♡	2♠	3◇
NB (b)	NB (c)	3♠	NB (c)
NB	Dbl	End	

(a) Could be a 3-card suit.
(b) I had already seen one of my partner's doubles.
(c) After a long hesitation.

Dummy went down with:

♠ A J 7 4
♡ Q 9 7 2
◇ 8
♣ K J 10 3

and ten tricks was the result. East was a little irate and the conversation with West went:

East: 'Why did you double?'
West: 'Because you hesitated.'
East: 'But you hesitated first, and anyway you didn't have a good enough hand. You know that you can only hesitate if you're strong!'

On the next deal we bid 6NT, and I laid the last five cards down claiming the contract, only to be told that the defenders could instruct me how to play it, and I would now go down as I was going to be instructed to play Kings under Aces. This brought the Director over, who agreed with my opponents!

I admitted that I didn't know the rules in Hong Kong, but maintained that in the UK I could not be forced to play stupidly. Eventually, the American Contract Bridge League's rules were produced, which coincide with ours, and 6NT was allowed to stand – but I was warned not to claim contracts in future because it 'confuses people'.

I did play at the Cricket Club again and, after the hustle and bustle of a long day in the office, it was always pleasant to be there. Everyone made me feel welcome – and I look back with pleasant memories on the incident of the 'Strong Pause'.

NEVER SAY DIE

BY TONY RICHARDS

Tales of the low life at local club duplicates usually go unrecorded. On the following hand declarer tried three throws of increasing desperation before emerging with a most undeserved good result:

♠ 3 2
♡ Q J 9 8 6 4
◊ Q 2
♣ Q J 5

	South	North
		NB
	1♠	2♡
	2NT	End

```
      N
 W         E
      S
```

♠ K J 8 6
♡ A 2
◊ A K
♣ 10 9 8 7 6

The bidding is not textbook: 1♠ was chosen as the opening bid, a) for pre-emptive effect, b) to claim the spade suit, and c) planning to rebid no-trumps over a red-suit response. Plan c) came into effect, but my wife now passed. Experience has taught her that, more often than not, I am not pleased to have no-trumps disturbed. We have the values for our bids, but there is the awful duplication in diamonds. Inevitably, a diamond is led.

After winning the first trick, the first try was the ♡A. The one legitimate play for the contract is to find the ♡K singleton with East, in which case a finesse against the Ten will bring in the heart suit. Needless to say, this only happens in Gold Cup finals or World Championships.

The next play is to continue with a small heart from hand, hoping that the King will be held up (this is the local duplicate). If the ♡Q is allowed to win and both opponents follow, a third round can be played, and the other top diamond discarded from declarer's hand. The defence must then either let dummy in with the ◊Q to make the good hearts or play on the black suits. In either case I may end up not many off. This try nearly worked – the ♡K was held up, but East discarded, so the unblocking play was not available.

Finally, real desperation sets in, and the ♣Q is played from dummy. Success! It is covered by the ♣K, West has the singleton Ace – and so the contract is now made with four tricks in clubs and two in each red suit. Marital bidding disagreements can be postponed for the moment.

SECOND PUZZLE

BY RICHARD WHEEN

In this double-dummy problem – which is slightly more difficult than my previous one on page 65 – North is to lead with clubs as trumps, and North–South are to make all six tricks against any defence.

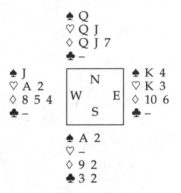

```
              ♠ Q
              ♡ Q J
              ◇ Q J 7
              ♣ –
  ♠ J         ┌─────────┐      ♠ K 4
  ♡ A 2       │    N    │      ♡ K 3
  ◇ 8 5 4     │ W     E │      ◇ 10 6
  ♣ –         │    S    │      ♣ –
              └─────────┘
              ♠ A 2
              ♡ –
              ◇ 9 2
              ♣ 3 2
```

Solution on page 215.

A PUZZLING PLAY

BY STEPHEN CASHMORE

During a recent practice of the Compass Team, Elizabeth (our best card-player, sitting East) explained something which had always puzzled me. I was South, as usual. My partner Norman (our strongest defender) sat North, and the team was completed by Wendy (our best bidder), sitting West.

♠ Q 6 5
♡ K J 7 2
♢ A 6 4
♣ J 9 7

```
      N
  W       E
      S
```

♠ A K 10 8 4
♡ Q 3
♢ K Q 9 5
♣ A 8

I opened 1♠. Norman responded 2NT. I rebid 3♢ and, after Norman corrected to 3♠, soon bid to 6♠. Wendy led the ♡10.

I had to lose the ♡A, and it seemed I was lucky to avoid a club lead which would have led to one down for sure. I played low on the heart lead – so did Elizabeth, and I won with the Queen. After drawing trumps, which were 3-2, I played a heart to the Jack and Ace. Elizabeth returned a club, I went up with the Ace, played the ♢K, then crossed to the ♢A (Elizabeth playing the ♢10) and discarded my losing club on the ♡K. Now all I had to do was find the diamonds right. I led my small diamond from dummy – but no luck! Elizabeth showed out. Wendy had started with ♢J–8–3–2, so I was one down after all.

'My hand!' claimed Elizabeth, meaning that she had 'fixed' this particular deal and was about to show me where I had gone wrong. We spread out the hands in silence.

'I had to knock out the ♡A for the club discard', I said.

'Right.'

'And he had to draw trumps, of course', remarked Norman.

'Wrong. After the hearts, draw only two rounds of trumps and then play off the top diamonds.'

'But someone might ruff', said Wendy, clearly puzzled.

'Then the contract was never making', said Elizabeth remorselessly.

I sighed. 'I've read about this in books', I told her, 'but I've never understood it.'

'Okay. Suppose the diamonds were 3–3. Draw two rounds of trumps and play the diamonds. It works, because nobody can ruff a diamond. You draw the last trump and claim. Agreed?'

We all nodded.

'Now suppose diamonds are 4–2. If you draw trumps, you go down. You've just proved that. What you have to do is try to ruff your fourth diamond. So – as before – draw two rounds of trumps and play the diamonds. If the person with the outstanding trump also has the four diamonds, you will be able to ruff your last diamond in peace. You take your ruff and then draw the last trump. It works – look at the cards. See?'

We all looked.

'But suppose the person with the *doubleton* diamond has three trumps and can ruff in?' complained Wendy.

'Then the contract can't be made', said Elizabeth. 'You can draw all the trumps, if you like, to prevent the ruff – but then you can't avoid losing the fourth diamond.'

She turned on me.

'Do you get it now?'

'I think so', I said slowly. 'For some reason it just seems... odd.'

Elizabeth was rearranging the cards.

```
   ♠ A K J 6 4   ┌───────┐   ♠ Q 10 3
   ♡ 5           │   N   │   ♡ A 9 7 2
   ◇ K 7 6 3     │ W   E │   ◇ A Q 8
   ♣ 8 5 2       │   S   │   ♣ J 4 3
                 └───────┘
```

'This was a question from a quiz', she said. 'West is in 4♠ and the lead is the ♡K. Take it from there.'

We all looked.

'There are nine top tricks', she added. 'The problem then is to find the tenth.'

'Isn't that always the way with problems', murmured Wendy, and I grinned at her.

'Dummy reversal', said Norman suddenly. 'If you ruff three hearts in hand, you can use the Ace, Queen and Ten to draw trumps. So you make six trump tricks instead of five. Is that right?'

Elizabeth nodded.

'More or less', she said. 'The official answer said: win with the ♡A. Ruff a heart. Play the ♠A, then cross to the ♠10. If trumps are 3-2, ruff another heart, cross to a top diamond, ruff the last heart, cross to the other top diamond, and draw the outstanding trump with the Queen. Now the ◇K is your tenth trick. Agreed?'

We played the hand through in our heads, Norman muttering to himself under his breath as if he had to say the cards to fix them in his mind. Eventually, we all agreed.

'But the official answer also said: if, after the ♠A and crossing to the ♠10, the trumps turn out to be 4–1, then just draw trumps and rely on the diamonds being 3–3. Now that I don't agree with. Do you see why?'

We all looked again, and suddenly I understood.

'It's like the fixed hand!' I exclaimed. 'If trumps are 4–1 you should play the top diamonds first anyway. You might be able to ruff the fourth one.'

'Exactly. If the diamonds are 3–3 it works. If the same defender holds both the trumps and diamonds it works. And if different defenders hold the diamonds and trumps you cannot make the contract however you play. Exactly!' repeated Elizabeth, and sat back with a satisfied expression on her face.

A CIVIL CONTRACT

On the way back from a Hubert Phillips match which her team had lost, the lady member purred: 'I don't wish to criticize, partner, but if you don't pass my 6♣ cue-bid, we might stand a better chance of reaching 7♡.'

'Is that what it was?' enquired the gentleman politely. 'I thought you were out of your depth, and passed to save you further embarrassment!'

SLAMS AND MORE SLAMS

BY GRAHAM HEDLEY

I read somewhere that on average there is a play for a slam on one in ten hands. This average did not apply to a recent local league match in which there were *eleven* slam hands in 24 boards. It has to be said, however, that neither side distinguished itself during the match with the accuracy either of the slam bidding or play, or defence. The results on the slam hands were as follows (the names of the players are omitted to protect the innocent).

Board No				Our score	IMPs
1	Us	6◇ ✓		+920	+15
	Oppo	6♣ - 6	(Played in cue-bid.)	+300	
2	Us	6♠ ✓	(Only 27 points, but a cold slam.)	+1430	+13
	Oppo	4♠ + 2		-680	
5	Us	6NT - 1	(Partner chose a 50% finesse,	-100	-13
	Oppo	3NT + 3	and not the 81% line.)	-690	
7	Us	4♡ + 2	(Missed the 21-points slam.)	+680	-7
	Oppo	4♠* + 1	(Not a good double!)	-990	
9	Us	3♠ - 1	(Missed the solid 6◇.)	-100	+7
	Oppo	5♡ - 4	(On way to 6◇ until 4♡ cue!)	+400	
11	Us	6♠ ✓	(Defence failed to cash A-K in	+980	+11
	Oppo	5♠ ✓	a side suit.)	-450	
12	Us	5♡ + 1	(Mis-bid cold 6♡.)	+480	+11
	Oppo	6♡ - 1	(Mis-played cold 6♡.)	+50	
15	Us	6◇ - 2	(Undisciplined overbidding.)	-200	-13
	Oppo	3NT ✓		-600	
17	Us	3NT + 3	(20-point hand with stiff ◇A	+690	+3
	Oppo	5◇ ✓	opposite 3◇ opener.)	-600	
19	Us	6♡ ✓	(We staggered into a 4–3 fit,	+980	+10
	Oppo	3NT + 3	did not find the good 6◇.)	-490	
24	Us	6NT - 1	(32 count, needs one finesse.)	-50	-11
	Oppo	3NT + 2	(Conservative, but successful.)	-460	

TOTAL IMPs ON SLAM HANDS (+70/-44). . . . . +26

Now for just one of the hands. This was Board 19:

Dealer: South
E/W Vul

```
                    ♠ 10 6
                    ♡ A Q 4
                    ◇ J 10 7 4
                    ♣ A Q 6 3
    ♠ Q 9 8 2              N         ♠ K 7 3
    ♡ 8 3                            ♡ 10 9 7 2
    ◇ 6 3          W           E     ◇ K 8 5
    ♣ K 10 9 8 5           S         ♣ J 7 2
                    ♠ A J 5 4
                    ♡ K J 6 5
                    ◇ A Q 9 2
                    ♣ 4
```

Our bidding was not of the best:

South	West	North	East
1♡	NB	2♣	NB
2◇	NB	4♡	NB
6♡	End		

This is not a pretty contract, but should always be made. I had the lead of the ♠2. After winning the King with my Ace, I returned a spade. West won, and switched to the ♣8. You can rise with the ♣A, return to hand via a diamond finesse (you have to take it sometime), and ruff the small spade in dummy. Then two top trumps, a second diamond finesse, draw trumps – and claim.

As I said, not a pretty contract. It is even less pretty on a club lead. Then you have to take a deep breath and play the ♣Q at trick one. I must ask partner why we could not play in 6◇. That is solid without a spade lead, and then relies on the diamond finesse.

CLUB COMPETITIONS

SLOW PLAYER OF THE YEAR: send your nominations for this award, a gold-plated tortoise, to the Secretary. (In your own good time, of course.)

(from The Barrivale Trump)

BULGARIA VS SCOTLAND

BY NEVENA DELEVA

In March 1993, the Scottish Bridge Union invited a Bulgarian ladies' team to play a series of friendly matches in Scotland. The Bulgarians won five of the six short matches against various Scottish ladies' teams, but more important was the experience gained by the Scottish squad members and the friendship which developed between the two groups of players. In May, a Scottish ladies' team visited Bulgaria to play in a major congress in Sofia, and they played a friendly match before the start of the official competition. The Bulgarian team was the one which was to represent their country in the European Championships in Menton, France, a month later. Again, it was Bulgaria who came out on top, though not by a large margin.

This was an interesting board, on which Bulgaria won 4 IMPs, though it could have been a lot more:

Dealer: South
Love All

```
                          ♠ 9 6 5 3
                          ♡ 10 8 6 4
                          ◊ K 9 4 3
                          ♣ 4
        ♠ 7 2                            ♠ A Q 8
        ♡ A K J 9              N          ♡ Q 7 5 2
        ◊ -              W          E     ◊ Q 10 7 2
        ♣ A K J 9 8 7 6          S        ♣ 10 3
                          ♠ K J 10 4
                          ♡ 3
                          ◊ A J 8 6 5
                          ♣ Q 5 2
```

Open Room:

South	West	North	East
Deleva	Grant	Popova	Onions
1◊ (a)	Dbl	NB	2♡
NB	4◊ (b)	NB	4♠ (c)
NB	4NT (d)	NB	5◊ (e)
NB	5NT (f)	NB	7♡
End			

(a) Precision. 11–15 points, may be short diamonds.
(b) Splinter bid agreeing hearts.
(c) Cue-bid, showing first-round control.
(d) Ace-asking.
(e) One Ace.
(f) Asking for the trump Queen.

Closed Room:

South	West	North	East
Adamson	Todorova	McQuaker	Garvalova
1◇	Dbl	2◇	2NT
NB	3♣ (a)	NB	3♡
NB	4◇ (b)	NB	4♡
End			

(a) 16+ points, natural.
(b) Cue-bid, agreeing hearts.

Quite a difference in evaluation by the two East–West pairs, and a major swing looked inevitable.

In the Open Room. I led my singleton heart against 7♡, and even playing double dummy declarer could not overcome the 4–1 trump break. He won in dummy, drew two more rounds of trumps, and played the ♣A–K. North ruffed, forced dummy with a diamond, and declarer ended up four down for minus 200.

In the Closed Room, Sheila Adamson led her fourth-highest diamond, declarer discarding from dummy, and North winning the King and returning the suit. Garvalova ruffed in dummy, took two rounds of trumps, then played the top clubs, only to find that she was one down as North ruffed – minus 50.

How should East play 4♡ after the bidding in the Closed Room? The easiest way is that when North wins the first trick, declarer should trust South for her opening bid and rely on the club finesse, as only 11 high-card points are missing. So East can ruff the second diamond, draw three rounds of trumps, cross to hand with the ♠A, draw the last trump, and take the club finesse, making twelve tricks.

If declarer suspects South of opening with fewer than 11 HCPs, i.e. with something like ♠K J 10 4 ♡3 ◇A J 8 6 5 3 ♣5 2, then the above is not a safe way to play 4♡. But South must surely hold the ◇A, so when North returns a low diamond at trick two, East covers and lets South win the trick. The best South can do is to play the ◇A to force dummy. Now declarer plays the ♡A and the ♣A–K, Whoever ruffs, East is in control: she wins a spade or diamond continuation in hand, crosses to dummy with a trump, ruffs a club high, and returns to dummy while drawing the last trump. This line succeeds whenever hearts are no worse than 4–1 and clubs 3–1.

COMBINE YOUR CHANCES

BY MIKE WHITTAKER

When you happen to be declarer you might quickly spot a line of play which, if successful, will allow you to make the contract. On closer examination of the cards, an alternative line of play might become obvious – one that offers a better chance of success. Before you embark on this improved line, and mentally congratulate yourself for having found it, you should give a good deal of thought towards trying to *combine* both of the two possibilities. If you can manage this, you will find that the 'hybrid' combination will give a better chance of success than any single line on its own.

So much for the theory. See if you can put it into practice on the hand below. You are South, playing in 6NT, and West leads the ♣5:

♠ A Q 7 4 3
♡ J 10 8
◇ A 3
♣ 10 9 7

```
        N
   W         E
        S
```

♠ K 2
♡ A 9 5 2
◇ K Q 7 2
♣ A K Q

Your first move is to count the number of top tricks. There are three each in spades, diamonds, and clubs, and the ♡A, making a total of ten. Where can the two extra tricks required come from?

Your first idea might be to play on spades. If the outstanding spades are split 3-3 you will have five spade tricks and will make your contract easily. But this is not the best of chances. It's more likely that the missing spades will be split 4–2 (48%) rather than 3–3 (36%).

The heart suit also offers the chance of extra tricks. The only top hearts that you are missing are the ♡K and ♡Q, and you can plan to take two finesses, hoping that East holds at least one of the missing honours. This is a much better line of play, for it will fail only when West holds both the ♡K–Q, giving you about a 75% chance of success.

Having identified two possible lines of play, don't just settle for the better one. Instead, you should think about combining them. It is very important to plan the order in which the cards are to be played. If you begin by playing three rounds of spades and find them to be splitting 4–2, it will probably be too late to turn to the hearts. Similarly, if you decide to go ahead with two finesses in hearts, it would be annoying to find West with both the ♡K and ♡Q, and then discover that the spades were actually splitting 3–3 all along!

The best line of play involves combining your chances in *both* spades *and* hearts as follows. After winning the club lead in hand, play a diamond to dummy's Ace. Lead the ♡J from dummy, letting it run if East plays low. Assuming that West wins this trick with the ♡K or ♡Q, you win whatever West returns and *now* try the spades to see how they split. If they are 3–3, then you have your twelve tricks. If not, you return to the heart suit and take a second finesse.

This line of play combines the chance of an even spade split with the chance of finding the heart honours divided, or both with East, and gives an overall chance of success of around 84% – clearly better than either of the two individual lines on their own.

BRIDGE APPLICATIONS

Antal Ja'rai, a member of the Hungarian National Bridge Team, is a lecturer at Budapest University. When his students sit their final exams, they are set questions to choose from: the selection is made by drawing a card from a pack incorporating three jokers, but no court cards. The numbered cards select the numbered questions, the jokers allow the student a free choice.

BRIDGE IN THE WILLOWS

BY BILL (BADGER) STARR

The Corbett Arms Hotel in Tywyn hosts not only bridge holidays, but also regular bridge courses throughout the year. Ever since I have been teaching there, I have been telling my pupils that, if they have a problem on a particular hand, they should record it, or make a note of the board number, and have a word with me afterwards.

Occasionally, they do, but one particular person (whom we shall call 'Fieldmouse') has a habit of producing something like this: 'Do you remember the hand where there is Ace-King and five spades, King-Jack and a couple of hearts, the ◊Q, and a few clubs? Well, what should my partner have answered when I bid 1♠?'

To begin with, I have counted at least fifteen cards, but by now her partner – shall we say, the 'Weasel' – has intervened with, 'You didn't bid a spade, you doubled the opponent's opening bid!' 'No, no, you've got it wrong', says Fieldmouse, 'you were the dealer and you passed, and the next hand bid…well, yes, anyway – you do remember the hand, don't you?'

This is an appeal to me, and no, I don't remember the hand – but usually with help from Mole and Rat I come up with a reconstruction and provide an answer. I am sure that every Improver should carry either an *Acol Diary* with those delightful blanks to record hands, or at least a pencil and paper!

However, one hand came up recently during one of our holidays, which needed no pencil and paper to be remembered forever. I held:

♠ A K x x
♡ A x x
◊ x x
♣ A K x x

My partner opened 1♡ and, just as I was getting ready to respond 2♣, Right-Hand Opponent bid 3♣! What should I have done now? We were vulnerable and they were not. Mole and I play a Negative Double up to 2♠, so I finally decided to bid 4♣. Mole duly alerted and bid 5♣ so, assuming that he must have something in diamonds – after all, he did open – I bid 6♣ which, on the lead of the ♠Q, duly made.

Our opponents were not amused, as between them they had the Ace and King of diamonds. They were even less amused when I proffered my piece of advice: avoid pre-empts, as they rarely disrupt competent opposition, and often get you into more trouble than they are worth!

HISTORY AT YOUR FINGERTIPS

BY GUY BERESINER

Bridge and playing-cards seem so perfect for one another, that it would probably not surprise you if I suggested that playing-cards were designed especially for this game.

In fact, the format of the deck of cards we know today is identical to those with which our ancestors played over five hundred years ago – a few centuries before bridge was invented. And this may be an underestimate: there are no records in existence that categorically state when playing-cards first made their appearance in England.

The first written mention we have of cards is in an Act of Parliament of 1463, forbidding their importation from foreign countries. If you consider that they must have been around for some time before being deemed important enough to be the subject of legislation, then you can estimate that their first introduction to this country must have been considerably earlier. The most solid evidence points to the French having introduced us to playing-cards, not least since our court cards today are not much different from their designs of the mid- to late-fifteenth century.

Once arrived in this country, playing-cards became instantly notorious. By comparison to the other popular pastime of the period, chess, they offered games of frenetic pace, invariably linked to that most addictive of vices – gambling. No-one was immune to their magnetism, and it did not take long before steps had to be taken to try and quell the rage for card-games. In 1495, for example, King Henry VII himself had to issue an edict forbidding his servants and apprentices from playing with cards except during the Christmas Holidays – certainly he was only too aware of their distracting powers, for among his private expenses at the time are several entries for losses at cards.

The effort to subdue the national passion for this new plaything was largely ineffectual, until some entrepreneurial spirit in the Court awakened to the idea that their popularity could actually be harnessed to make money for the Crown – a Bill was swiftly passed through Parliament, and soon a tax was slapped on the making of playing-cards.

It is estimated that the first taxes on playing-cards were levied in the mid- to late-sixteenth century, during Queen Elizabeth's reign. Evidently Her Majesty was no mean business-woman – she granted a monopoly in card-making to Ralph Bowles and then, in return for royal protection from imported cards, promptly demanded a 'recompense' of three shillings per gross, or a farthing a pack. It is recorded that this arrangement generated around £5000 per annum for the Crown; at that rate, some 4,800,000 packs must have been produced – a testimony to how the popularity of playing-cards had developed. The Crown was delighted by this new source of income.

Later, while Queen Anne was reigning and conflict with Spain was imminent, it became evident that more funds would be needed to finance the war effort. It did not take long to work out where these funds would come from: the tax on cards duly rocketed to three pence a pack. With the wholesale price of a deck at the time being a penny-ha' penny, there was something of an outcry from card-making circles. However, it all fell on deaf ears: clearly exhilarated by the success of this tax, the powers-that-were doubled it in 1711 to sixpence a pack, and the increase went up periodically until 1801, when it peaked at three shillings a pack.

You might be wondering at this stage how exactly tax was collected on playing-cards. The sophistication of VAT accounting did not exist at the time, and tax-dodging must have been a prolific pastime. Initially, the system was that one of the cards – usually the Ace of Spades – was officially stamped to indicate that tax had been paid.

In 1765 the Ace became the obligatory 'duty card' when a new method was introduced. The Stamp Office would keep a stock of pre-stamped Aces of Spades, and card-makers were instructed to print their decks short of that one crucial card. When the tax for the packs was paid, the Office issued the Ace of Spades to complete the pack, and the deck could be sold. To seal the effectiveness of this system, the forging of the Ace of Spades, the only way to escape paying tax, was made a capital offence – another sign of how important this source of revenue had become.

The tax was only abolished as recently as 1960, by when the duty was back down to three pence a pack, and seen as more trouble to the Inland Revenue than was worth bothering with. Today, most packs still display an ornate Ace of Spades of the manufacturer's design in recognition of this aspect of the history of playing-cards.

Apart from the Ace of Spades, which is generally individual to the manufacturer who makes the deck, little has changed in the design of the cards we use today from the ones first introduced to us by the French. The English tendency to abhor change meant that practical developments in playing-cards that appeared on the Continent, such as the introduction of double-headed figures in the mid-nineteenth century, were enthusiastically resisted in this country until stuffy principles had to give way to common sense, some forty years after everyone else had caught on.

Most other cornerstones in the evolution of playing-cards were similarly practical modifications, and appeared in the few years either side of 1880 – the introduction of rounded corners, corner indices, and thinner cards to facilitate shuffling. And finally, we are indebted to the Americans for introducing to us the need for a Joker, which is used for their game of *Euchre*. Originally, the Joker was just a blank extra card in a pack, but later it was seen as an opportunity for a little expression. Today, there are many people who only collect the Jokers, and discard the rest of the pack!

Through all these changes, however, the most complex part of the pack, the court card designs, have remained largely faithful to the original French style. The apparel is typical of English dress of the sixteenth century, but the postures and even expressions on the court cards are unchanged. This may be due to the belief that alterations to these most important cards would incite bad luck – and any manufacturer who dared add a bit of individuality to their packs found that sales plummeted.

Essentially, therefore, the cards we use today are the same as those with which our ancestors played. So next time, rather than slamming down the cards as you defeat declarer's contract, try and be a little more gentle – after all, you are handling over five hundred years of history.

EAVESDROPPINGS

North: 'Can I get you a coffee during the interval?'
South: 'No, thanks – it might keep me awake.'

(from the NCBA newsletter)

DID YOU SCRAPE A WIN?

BY BERNARD MAGEE

You are playing in a top-flight teams match over 64 boards. After 40, your team is 16 IMPs down. You progress through the last set of boards, which seems to be too flat until you bid a 3NT which goes one off – a little too tight! Two hands to go – a doubled part-score three off must be a good score, but surely you are still losing.

Then this – holding the West hand below, you hear this auction:

South	West	North	East
			3♣
4♣ (a)	NB	4♠	NB
5♡	NB	6♡	End

(a) Strong take-out.

You decide to lead your singleton club (after all, it is partner's suit), and dummy comes down with:

```
          ♠ A K Q 10 5
          ♡ 10 2
          ◊ J 10 7
          ♣ J 6 5
♠ J 7 2        ┌─────────┐
♡ Q 6 3        │    N    │
◊ Q 6 5 4 3 2  │ W     E │
♣ 8            │    S    │
               └─────────┘
```

Quite a few tricks! Your ♣8 is covered by the Jack, Queen, and Ace. Declarer lays down the ♡A, drawing your partner's ♡J. Plan your defence.

Solution on page 216.

Solution on page 216.

ON THE CHARING CROSS LINE

'Only game calls after London Bridge!'

UTTER DISASTER

BY GEOFF HALLIDAY

Dealer: West
Game All

```
                              ♠ Q
                              ♡ A 10 6 5
                              ◇ A 8 6 5
                              ♣ K J 10 3
        ♠ A K J 10 7 3                      ♠ 2
        ♡ K J              N                ♡ Q 9 8 4 3
        ◇ 4 2         W         E           ◇ Q 10 9 7 3
        ♣ A Q 8            S                ♣ 6 5
                              ♠ 9 8 6 5 4
                              ♡ 7 2
                              ◇ K J
                              ♣ 9 7 4 2
```

South	West	North	East
	1♠	Dbl	2◇
NB	2♠	NB	NB
Dbl	End		

I was in the South seat when this hand cropped up in an Aggregate Pairs event. East's take out into 2◇ rather than 2♡ was a little odd, and my double, which closed the bidding, was probably ill-judged.

The book lead would, I imagine, be the ♠Q, and correct defence sets the contract one down. On a diamond lead to the Jack and a trump return, the contract goes one off if declarer rises with the ♣A at trick two – and might even go two down if the ♣10 is finessed.

In the event the hand proved disastrous for the defence. North led a small club! Declarer won the ♣A–Q, ruffed a third round with dummy's singleton trump, and led a heart to his King, which was allowed to hold. Five rounds of spades followed and North, embarrassed for discards, threw his remaining club and three diamonds in order to protect his hearts. In hand with the ♠9, I led the ◇J, overtaken by North's Ace. In desperation, he now cashed the ♡A and dummy took the ♡Q leaving declarer with a trump for the last trick. So 2♠ doubled and made with two overtricks gave the fine score of 1070, a swing of 1270 (or 1570, depending on whether the contract goes one or two down).

Of additional interest (or is it just in order to torture myself?) is the fact that with careful timing a 3♣ contract can be made on the North–South cards!

GOLDEN OLDIES

BY NORMAN MACKENZIE

Aberdeen Bridge Club recently celebrated its sixtieth anniversary, and a feature of the event was a tournament of hands first played sixty years ago in the 'Second (Empire) Bridge International' between a team representing the North-East of Scotland, captained by George MacPhee, and a team representing England captained by the redoubtable Col. Walter Buller CBE. England won the match by a margin of 3630 points. Captain Ewart Kempson was a member of the English team and, following the match, he edited a book, *Bridge Contest at Aberdeen*, commenting on the one hundred hands played.

Twenty-four of these hands were selected for the Anniversary Tournament, and the results from the 1933 match and the 1993 tournament make interesting comparisons. If some of the 1933 bidding appears a trifle strange, I should explain that the match was essentially a contest between the Approach Forcing System played by the Scottish team, and the so-called Natural Bidding System played by the English team.

Dealer: South
Love All

```
                        ♠ 10 8 3
                        ♡ 7
                        ◇ A 10 9 6 3 2
                        ♣ A Q 7
    ♠ 9 4                               ♠ K J 7 5 2
    ♡ A K Q J 10 5      N              ♡ 9 8 6 4 3 2
    ◇ 5 4           W       E          ◇ —
    ♣ 6 4 2             S              ♣ 9 5
                        ♠ A Q 6
                        ♡ —
                        ◇ K Q J 8 7
                        ♣ K J 10 8 3
```

This was undoubtedly the Hand of the Match when it was played in 1933, and I expected some fireworks when I included it in the Anniversary Tournament. The bidding in the original match was as follows:

Room 1

South	West	North	East
Mr MacPhee	Col. Buller	Mr Davidson	Capt. Kempson
1◊	1♡	4◊	4♡
5◊	5♡	6◊	6♡
Dbl	End		

Room 2

South	West	North	East
Mr Mathieson	Mrs MacPhee	Mrs Evers	Mr Paton
2◊	2♡	4◊	4♡
6◊	NB	NB	6♡
NB	NB	7◊	NB
NB	7♡	Dbl	End

Nine tricks made in both rooms.

At both tables, East–West sacrificed against the slam, although at Table 1 Ewart Kempson wasn't faced with the traumatic decision of sacrificing against the grand. George MacPhee's wife, Mildred, was an extremely accomplished player, but this was the first hand she ever played in match play. One can only imagine the doubts she must have experienced before making her bid of 7♡. Was she making a phantom sacrifice, or was 7◊ really makeable? As you can see, 7◊ makes against any lead, and Mrs MacPhee showed splendid judgement in producing her amazing sacrifice bid.

How would present-day players fare? In the Anniversary Tournament the hand was played fifteen times. One North–South was allowed to play in 7◊, six were allowed to play in 6◊, and six were content to play in 5◊. Only two East–West pairs played in hearts, one in 5♡ and the other in 6♡. Both came down earning joint tops for their enterprise (or good fortune!).

Dealer: North
Love All

```
                      ♠ A Q 10 6 5 4 2
                      ♡ 5
                      ◊ A 10 9 4
                      ♣ 7
        ♠ J 9 7                        ♠ –
        ♡ 10 6 3          N            ♡ Q J 9 8 2
        ◊ K Q 8 5     W       E        ◊ 7 3 2
        ♣ Q J 6          S            ♣ K 9 8 5 3
                      ♠ K 8 3
                      ♡ A K 7 4
                      ◊ J 6
                      ♣ A 10 4 2
```

Another example of good judgement on the part of the 'Golden Oldies' is shown by the hand at the bottom of page 139:

Room 1

South	West	North	East
		3♠	NB
4♡	NB	4♠	NB
6♠	End		

Room 2

South	West	North	East
		2♠	NB
4NT	NB	5♠	NB
6♠	End		

When this hand was played in our Anniversary Event, only three North–South pairs bid to 6♠ – although one foolhardy pair bid to 7♠ going one down.

Although sometimes lacking in science, players in 1933 seemed to have the knack of reaching the best contract almost intuitively, and an analysis of all the tournament hands shows that they would give a very good account of themselves if matched against their modern counterparts.

EAVESDROPPINGS

At a recent National event, one player was constantly engaged in a loud commentary on his partner's shortcomings. When the crescendo had reached its peak, a calm voice was heard from a nearby table:
  'Do excuse us if our bridge disturbs your post-mortem!'

DISMAL DENIS

BY JIMMY ALLAN

Dismal Denis, wending his way towards our table in the coffee room seemed so despondent that were it anyone else we could have sensed some national disaster. Too late I realized that it was the morning after the weekly duplicate tournament – DD had already seized my prescription pad and was writing down these hands:

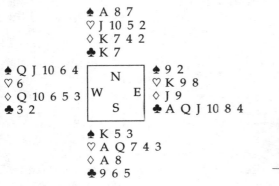

'Just how unlucky can anyone be! I am in a 4♡ contract, the heart finesse is right – no problem – but that stupid O'Leary, instead of leading the ♠Q, led the ♣3. I lost two club tricks, then on the ♣J O'Leary fumbled with his cards, peered over his spectacles – and trumped! He immediately apologized for such stupidity – but you can see what happened. I had to overruff with the ♡10, and now lost a trump trick as well as a spade trick to go one light.'

Our quiet radiologist thought that East should have returned the ♣4 – forcing O'Leary to ruff – but added that even the waitress would still have made the contract.

This was too much for DD. He called Millie to the table and gave her the problem: '♣A, ♣Q, ♣4 ruffed on your left with the ♡6.'

'I overruff with the ♠7,' quoth Millie.

DD's snort of disgust was quickly silenced by the radiologist. 'Quite correct, Millie. You throw the losing spade. Now you have no problem in making the remainder of the tricks!'

THE UNASSUMING CUE-BID

BY DEREK PATTERSON AND MARK HOWARTH

When the Battle of the Baize is finally won and the enemy routed, let us drop in on the victory celebrations. What do we see? All the conventions and system-bids are there, boasting of the part they've played.

Weak No-trump and Limit Raises are claiming their usual amount of credit. The aristocratic Count Signal boasts of masterminding the entire defence, whilst Weak Jump Overcall is telling the world how he kept the enemy out of game. Now we see the two Blackwoods – the urbane, sophisticated Roman Key Card and his rather more agricultural brother, Simple Blackwood.

A small group lingers in the background, shying away from the public declamations of others. Noticeable amongst these is the rather quiet Unassuming Cue-bid, diffident as befits his name. UCB (as his friends call him) is far too modest to push himself forward, but represents one of the most useful and flexible weapons available to a modern bridge player.

Sometimes our appreciation of any method is enhanced by being made aware of its fringe benefits. By way of illustration, let us assume a typical evening at the club. Your partner has failed to turn up. You consider going home, but the thought of being subjected to another pitiful display by the England football team is distinctly unpleasant. You decide to kibitz.

♠ A 8 5
♡ K Q 4 3
◇ 5 4 2
♣ 9 6 2

South	North
1◇	1♡
2♣	2◇
3◇	3NT

♠ 9
♡ A 8
◇ A K Q J 8 6
♣ J 10 7 5

The first hand you see involves North–South bidding these cards to 3NT, following the auction as described. Not exactly thrilling stuff, but a competent sequence nevertheless.

Later in the evening, your attention is drawn by raised voices – well, at least one. Being less than superhuman, you wander over to investigate. You are surprised to see that it is the hand above that has caused such consternation. This time, North–South have climbed to an unsuccessful 5◊ contract, and declarer is not best pleased. 'Bidding on tram tickets… you're lucky I didn't double…' etc.

It turns out that the auction has been:

South	West	North	East
1◊	1♠	Dbl	3♠
?			

North's double, of the Sputnik variety, could hardly be criticized, but South now had a very awkward problem. He had a good hand, but there was no room left for exploring the best spot. In between splutters and threatening to bite off the end of his pipe, South is now expounding upon the difficulties of trying to make sensible bids against people who 'bid on rubbish' and are 'very lucky'.

However, East–West do not look like people who have just been 'very lucky'. Indeed, South's claim that a smart double would have wiped the smile off their faces is incorrect, for 3♠ would have been just one down – cheap at the price. Consider the full deal:

```
Dealer: South          ♠ A 8 5
Game All               ♥ K Q 4 3
                       ◊ 5 4 2
                       ♣ 9 6 2
   ♠ K 10 7 4 2    ┌──────────┐    ♠ Q J 6 3
   ♥ J 9 6         │    N     │    ♥ 10 7 5 2
   ◊ 10 7 3        │  W    E  │    ◊ 9
   ♣ A K           │    S     │    ♣ Q 8 4 3
                   └──────────┘
                       ♠ 9
                       ♥ A 8
                       ◊ A K Q J 8 6
                       ♣ J 10 7 5
```

Note that the East hand is indeed light in terms of High-Card Points. Note, also, that it was the 3♠ bid that caused South's problem. Over a mere 2♠, South could have bid 3♠ himself, asking his partner for a stop. Was it a case of the wrong bid at the right time? Was East lucky? Not really.

You quiz the 'trouble-makers' and learn that the 3♠ bid was entirely pre-emptive, not a game invitation at all. East had merely followed the good principle of obstructive bidding by *raising to the level of the fit on a weak hand* (four trumps plus the expected five for the overcall equals nine, therefore bid to the three level – the level of nine tricks).

West explains: 'On all hands on which partner would have liked to invite game, he would have bid 2◇, an *Unassuming Cue-bid*, showing support for the overcall and at least 9 High-Card Points. Therefore, immediate raises of the overcalled suit are pre-emptive, with maybe 5–8 points and a bit of shape.'

So, in our round-about way, we have stumbled across the Unassuming Cue-bid.

How the UCB Works

By bidding the enemy suit at the lowest available level, the partner of the overcaller effects a UCB. By this means, he shows support for partner and a reasonable sprinkling of HCPs, perhaps 9 or more. He does not promise any particular holding in the enemy suit.

The UCB frees immediate trump raises for pre-emptive purposes. We have seen that this can be devastating. By making pre-emptive raises to the Level of the Fit responder combines pressure with reasonable safety. So, when the auction has started:

LHO	Partner	RHO	Responder
1◇	1♠	2♣	?

Responder can bid:

2◇ = Spade support, any hand which has a constructive feel to it. The bid is unlimited in strength, but has about 9 points as its lower limit.

2♠ = A weak raise, say 5–8 points, usually three-card support.

3♠ = A weak raise, say 5–8 points, usually four-card support.

4♠ = A weak raise, say 5–8 points, usually five-card support.

Continuation after a UCB

The overcaller bases his rebid on the assumption that the UCB has been made on a balanced hand with three-card support, and about 9–12 points. If game is unlikely, he signs off in the knowledge that partner will try again with a slightly stronger hand. Consider this auction:

LHO	Partner	RHO	Responder
1◇	1♠	2♣	2◇
NB	3♠		

The last bid invites responder to bid game with the equivalent of 11–12 points or better, and to pass with 9–10.

After South has opened 1♡, the recommended auction on the East–West hands below is as follows:

```
♠ A K 10 6 4        ┌─────────┐        ♠ J 8 7 2
♡ J 5               │    N    │        ♡ 6 3
♢ K 6            W  │         │  E      ♢ A Q J 5
♣ 8 6 5 2           │    S    │        ♣ A J 4
                    └─────────┘
```

South	West	North	East
1♡	1♠	NB	2♡
NB	2♠	NB	3♠
NB	4♠	End	

The overcall is as routine as, by now, is the UCB response. The over-caller cannot envisage game opposite a balanced three-card raise in the 9–12 zone. Hence, he rebids 2♠. Effectively, opener is stating that his hand is at best a minimum opener. Because responder is better than the aforementioned 9–12, another move is called for: 3♠ is a simple bid over which overcaller will pass if very weak, but bid game with a sound overcall. In fact, a better bid than 3♠ would be 3♢: the spade support has already been promised by the 2♡ bid, and 3♢ shows where responder's points are concentrated.

Because an overcall can be made on a very wide range of hands – from very weak (for example, ♠ K J x x x ♡ K x x ♢ x ♣ x x x x) up to pretty strong (say, ♠ A Q x x x ♡ A x x ♢ A x ♣ K x x) it is important from a constructive point of view that the limited space available is used intelligently. The UCB keeps the bidding low, conserving space for the maximum amount of information exchange. With any luck, game will be bid – or avoided – with a fair degree of certainty on any given deal.

Meanwhile, when game appears unlikely, we can consume bidding space by making a pre-emptive raise. Under such circumstances, it will be the opposition who will need the space for *their* information exchange – and it simply won't be there.

By incorporating the UCB into our armoury, we free immediate rais-es for pre-emptive purposes. Therefore, we can bid with accuracy when we wish, and make pressure bids should this seem more appropriate.

SPECTRE AT THE FEAST

BY MAUREEN DENNISON

An American friend of mine told me this plaintive tale, and I wrote it down for your amusement and education. Here it is, as it was told to me.

THE SPECTRE AT THE FEAST IS MURPHY

When you play for a first time with a new partner, irrespective of skills, styles, and abilities, the spectre at the feast is Murphy, and the practical issues at the table will be governed by Murphy's Law.

Murphy entered the scene at 6 p.m. three days before Christmas, in the shape of a good friend whose new baby had decided to come into the world two weeks early, on a night when he was scheduled to play an important knock-out handicap match. The festive season meant that he had been unable to enlist the help of friends and acquaintances of good playing standard, and at last he turned to me. Little did I realize I was to be the handicap! I was free, and I had to be at the venue by 7 p.m., a mere forty-five-minute drive away. I picked up a take-away hamburger, which exploded in the car, and I arrived dripping ketchup and lettuce – but my hosts assured me that they would not have noticed if I hadn't explained.

Only fifteen minutes late, but as I was playing with a quality partner, I was confident we would have no system problems, even without prior discussion. We agreed on *Bridge World* Standard as our basic system, and I agreed to Flannery, and got my partner to agree to Inverted Major Suit Raises with Fit-showing Jumps. Though not his normal style, he would have no problems. We didn't discuss Flannery, because everybody knows that. Murphy was sitting at our elbows waiting for his chance. He waited until the last hand of the first session before exerting his influence.

Partner opened 2◇, the Flannery bid to show a limited hand with 4–5 in the majors, and my hand was enormous:

♠ K 9 7 5
♡ J 10 9 4 2
◇ –
♣ K J 3 2

This looked like a bidding quiz problem. If partner had the ♠A–Q and the ♡A–K, a slam was certainly on. Suppose I start with 2NT, and partner bids the expected 3◇ – what could I do next? Bid 5♡? If 5♡ asks about hearts, does it ask about spades as well? I was in a dilemma. It could be an important hand – the other team had received a 21-IMP handicap, and it was an 11-IMP decision I was making.

Well, I finally decided I couldn't find out enough to make any slam decisions from my side of the table, so I was just about to blast 4♡ when Murphy rushed in to help me. The answer was the *Splinter Bid of 4◇*. I know you agree a suit when you make a splinter, but partner should realize I would have support for both majors.

I have since asked a lot of people what they thought my bid showed. The answers ranged from a Transfer, a good diamond suit, Roman Key-card Blackwood – but there was not the suggestion of a splinter bid amongst them. I gave everybody partner's hand to see what they would have bid. This is what he held:

♠ Q J 8 4
♡ A Q 7 6 3
◇ K Q 2
♣ 5

The bids selected ranged from 4♡ to 6◇. One person said: 'Undiscussed bids always seem clearer to the player making the bid than to the partner who is receiving the information.' I will remember that.

The result? Are you interested in the result? We were 44 IMPs down at half-time – and my partner did comment gently that 3–0 trump fits are difficult to handle at the four level from his side of the table.

A HISTORY OF BRIDGE COMPUTERS

BY ANDY ROLAND

The first bridge computer to appear on the British market was the Fidelity *Bridge Challenger* in the early 1980s. This device assumed that the player(s) had a pack of cards, which they dealt face down and then passed through an optical scanning device that was part of the *Bridge Challenger*. The computer then communicated with its users by means of a one-line LCD screen.

The first portable bridge computer appeared on the market in the mid-eighties. *Play Bridge*, as it was called, consisted of a single LCD screen and was only able to show two hands at a time – an advance on the *Bridge Challenger* – i.e. the human player's hand and the dummy. Play was indescribably poor, and that the product sold very well was only due to its novelty value.

Further variations appeared on the market over the next few years. In particular the *BG2* and the *Pro Bridge 100* sold well, and played bridge up to the standard of a fairly-poor bridge-club player. The screen and graphics were expanded, so that they were much easier to read than hitherto. They also had the useful feature that two could be linked together, allowing two players to play against the computer.

In the early 1990s, Saitek, who were now the only manufacturers in the bridge-computer business, brought out the *Pro Bridge 310*, a portable , and the *Pro Bridge 510*, a table-top. The standard of bridge offered was greatly superior to any previous models, and for the benefit of the British bridge-playing public, the program included the Acol system. In addition, these two computers could be connected together to allow two players to challenge the computer itself.

The *Pro Bridge 510* also contains an update facility, such that more advanced bridge programs can be added by the owner, at relatively low cost, to take advantage of any developments which no doubt will take place in the future.

This article is reprinted from The 1994 Collins Bridge Diary by kind permission of the publishers.

A BIDDING QUIZ

BY ANDREW KAMBITES

All the questions below feature this hand. You are East at Love All, playing duplicate pairs.

♠ J
♡ Q 10 9 5 3
◊ A J 6 3 2
♣ 8 2

1) What is your response if partner opens with these bids:
   (a) 1♣?   (b)1◊?   (c) 1♡?   (d)1♠?

2) Playing a completely natural system (with no two-suited overcalls available) what should East bid after these sequences?

	South	West	North	East
(a)	South	West	North	East
			1◊	?
(b)	South	West	North	East
			1♠	?
(c)	South	West	North	East
	1♠	NB	NB	?
(d)	South	West	North	East
	1◊	NB	NB	?

Solutions on page 217.

THE DOLLE MINA COUP

BY GUSTAVU AGLIONE

Well, it was only to be expected. When Joyce Nicholson wrote *Why Women Lose at Bridge* in 1986, it was only a matter of time before someone wrote a reply. So, I was not surprised by the recent publication of *Why Women Win at Bridge* by Danny Roth.

That's what I tell Galina, but she does not seem to be impressed. She says, 'On earlier occasions I have shown you that boys and girls are different, and that's true also at the bridge table. We women are much smarter, of course, as can be seen from this deal:

```
♠ A                          ♠ Q 7
♡ 8 7 5 4 3        N         ♡ K 10 6
◇ 10 2          W     E      ◇ A K 8 6 5 3
♣ K Q J 10 4       S         ♣ A 3
```

'The auction is best forgotten, but there you are: you are West, declarer in 6♡, and North leads the ♠J. Tell me, what are your chances? Do you see any whatsoever?'

No, I do not see any possibility of landing this slam, and that's what I tell Galina – with some hesitation, though, because I am afraid of a hidden snag which I may have overlooked.

She nods and continues: 'Yes, a very masculine assessment. Zero-per-cent chance of making your contract, because when you miss the A–Q–J–9–x of trumps you will have at least two losers in the suit and that is one too many for a successful small slam.

'Ina Oofthoven, the famous feminist bridge-writer and international player for New South Domina, however, when playing this hand had very different ideas. After a gracious, 'Thank you, partner!' she covered the ♠J lead with the ♠Q and took South's ♠K with her Ace. Then she continued with the ♣A, ♣K, and ♣Q, as though she was aiming at discarding the ♠7 in dummy, which looked very much like a loser to North who ruffed the third round of clubs with the ♡9. Ina overruffed with dummy's ♡10, then ruffed the ♠7 in hand and led a small

150

heart to the King. This reduced the total number of losers in the trump suit to one, since this was the complete layout:'

```
                    ♠ J 10 9 3
                    ♡ A 9 2
                    ◊ Q 9 7 4
                    ♣ 6 2
    ♠ A                              ♠ Q 7
    ♡ 8 7 5 4 3        N             ♡ K 10 6
    ◊ 10 2         W       E         ◊ A K 8 6 5 3
    ♣ K Q J 10 4       S             ♣ A 3
                    ♠ K 8 6 5 4 2
                    ♡ Q J
                    ◊ J
                    ♣ 9 8 7 5
```

Galina smiles shyly, then she says: 'Yes, that's the female touch: pretend to do something as naïve as covering the ♠J with the ♠Q, and then cajoling North into shortening his trump holding. Simple – and since "Women's Lib" in your country is called the "Dolle Mina" movement, let us give Ina's play the great Dutch name of the "Dolle Mina" Coup!'

A POLITE REPLY

A 19-year-old was directing for the first time at a duplicate session in his local club. As soon as he settled down, the cry of 'Director!' was heard. 'I have only twelve cards!', announced a lady in plaintive tones.

'Madam', was the polite reply, 'you must be very disappointed!'

A SPONSOR'S VIEWPOINT

BY STEPHEN DABBY

The London-based firm of Chartered Accountants, Alan & Co., chose the 1992 Brighton Swiss Teams to launch into sports sponsorship. The firm chose bridge both because of the significant numbers of bridge players amongst accountants, particularly tax specialists, and because they felt happy identifying Alan & Co. with the image of Bridge as an activity.

The Alan & Co. team of Beryl Kerr, Mike Scoltock, Martin Garvey and John Howard cut a colourful splash in the day-glo Alan & Co. T-shirts. The following hands demonstrate that the team certainly had a lively weekend.

♠ J 8 5
♡ 10 9 6
◇ Q 6 2
♣ K J 7 4

The first one is a lead problem. Holding these cards, what do you lead as West after the auction below? Check at the end of this article to see if you've found the killing lead.

North	South	
1♡	2♠	(a) Blackwood, asking for Aces
3◇	4NT (a)	(b) 0 or 4
5♣ (b)	5NT (c)	(c) Blackwood, asking for Kings
6◇ (d)	6NT	(d) One

The second deal demonstrates the modern cavalier attitude to the case of Weak Twos:

```
                    ♠ A 10 7 4 3
                    ♡ 9 6
                    ◇ J 6
                    ♣ J 9 8 4
♠ Q J 6 2        ┌──────────┐        ♠ -
♡ Q 5            │    N     │        ♡ A 10 8
◇ A Q 10 9 4   W │        E │ E      ◇ 7 5 3 2
♣ K Q            │    S     │        ♣ A 10 7 6 5 3
                 └──────────┘
                    ♠ K 9 8 5
                    ♡ K J 7 4 3 2
                    ◇ K 8
                    ♣ 2
```

At the table where the Alan & Co. team were sitting East–West, the bidding went:

South	West	North	East
	Howard		Garvey
		2♠ (!)	Dbl (!)
4♠	Dbl (a)	NB	5♣
NB	6◊	End	

(a) Responsive

Declarer ruffed the ♠A lead, took the diamond finesse, drew trumps, and established the clubs for thirteen tricks.

At the other table, matters took a different turn:

South	West	North	East
Scoltock		Kerr	
		NB	NB
2♡	Dbl	NB	3♣
NB	3◊	NB	3♡
NB	3♠	NB	5◊
End			

Declarer won the opening heart lead in dummy and played a diamond to the Ace. An attempt to unblock the ♣K–Q led to South ruffing and promoting North's ◊J with a third round of hearts – 5◊ minus one.

Back to our lead problem. This was the full deal:

Dealer: North
Game All
6NT by South

```
                    ♠ 9
                    ♡ K Q 8 5 4 2
                    ◊ J 9 7 4 3
                    ♣ Q
    ♠ J 8 5                        ♠ Q 10 6 2
    ♡ 10 9 6          N            ♡ 7
    ◊ Q 6 2       W       E        ◊ 10 8
    ♣ K J 7 4         S            ♣ 10 9 8 6 5 3
                    ♠ A K 7 4 3
                    ♡ A J 3
                    ◊ A K 5
                    ♣ A 2
```

Mike Scoltock found the killing lead: the ♣K!

IN THE MIDDLE OF THE NIGHT

BY STEIN AKER

The scene is a cottage called 'Kramboden' in the mountains surrounding Bergen on the west coast of Norway, five or six years ago. As happy (bridge) students, we used to gather there once a year for a Bridge Marathon Pairs event – seventeen hours of play without a single break! On this occasion, my partner Bjorn and I were moving towards top position when, at 3.30 a.m., I picked up the South hand below. I opened 1♡, and the bidding proceeded:

♠ A 10 9 6 3
♡ 10 9 2
◊ 5 4
♣ K 10 8

South	West	North	East
Stein	Trond	Bjorn	Ulf
1♡	NB	1♠	NB
3◊	NB	3♡	NB
4♡	Dbl	End	

```
    N
W       E
    S
```

♠ J
♡ A K 7 5 4
◊ K Q J 9
♣ A J 3

Trond led the ♠8; I looked at the dummy with pleasure, won with the ♠A (Ulf encouraging from the East seat), then tried a diamond to the King. Trond grabbed his Ace and exited with the ♠2, confirming that the opening lead was from a doubleton. I inserted dummy's ♠10, Ulf covered with the ♠Q, and I ruffed. Now I played the ♡A and East threw a spade – giving me the bad news that West had started with five trumps. It looked as though I would have to lose three heart tricks for one down.

Quite worried, I decided to play Trond for the ♣Q. I laid down the ♣J, Trond ducking smoothly. I closed my eyes and let it ride – sighing with relief when East followed with a small club. Then I cashed the two top diamonds, discarding a spade from dummy, and continued with the ♣A on which Trond played the ♣Q. This was the end position:

```
              ♠ 9 6
              ♡ 10 9
              ◇ –
              ♣ K
  ♠ –                        ♠ K 7
  ♡ Q J 8 6    ┌─────────┐   ♡ –
  ◇ –          │    N    │   ◇ 10
  ♣ 7          │ W     E │   ♣ 9 4
               │    S    │
               └─────────┘
              ♠ –
              ♡ K 7 5
              ◇ 9
              ♣ 3
```

Once again, I held my breath, and put the ♣3 on the table. Trond followed and dummy's King won. Now a spade ruffed with the ♡K (Trond underruffing with the ♡6), then the ◇9 promoting a trump trick in dummy – and West's three trump tricks had shrunk to two! Ten tricks for a clear top.

We didn't win the tournament, but this deal made my night – or rather, the early hours of the morning!

THE LEAGUE MUST GO ON

On the morning of a match in the Yorkshire league, one member of a Malton team reporting sick with a temperature well into the 100s said she had also lost her voice.

'That's OK, dear', said the captain. 'we do use silent bidders, you know.'

Ken Hayton

THE HAND

BY DAVID PORISS

You are playing in a knock-out event at an ACBL Regional with a pick-up partner whom you and your team-mates have nicknamed 'Matilda the Hun'. The woman was a terror at the table. If I bid and made a difficult slam, she would say nothing – but I sure got an earful whenever I gave up one tiny overtrick. Unlike a regular one- or two-session event, I had to keep playing with this woman round after round. My team-mates refused to switch partners, and I refused to play bridge. Unfortunately, we kept winning.

I present this information solely as background for the following bridge movie* from a hand that occurred during the fifth round (semi-finals). You are South, vulnerable while the opponents are not, when you pick up this nice collection in fourth seat:

The bidding begins on your left with West the dealer:

♠ A K
♡ A J 10 x x
◊ A K 10 9 8
♣ x

West	North	East	South
NB	NB	2◊	?

The 2◊ is alerted and explained as Flannery, i.e. 11–15 points with 5 hearts and 4 spades. What is your bid?

Pass is acceptable, even 3◊ (you'll play it there), but I doubled. Whether you passed or doubled, your Left-Hand Opponent bids 2♡, and the bidding continues:

West	North	East	South
NB	NB	2◊	Dbl
2♡	NB	NB	?

What do you do now?

---

*A Bridge movie is a multi-part story that presents several bidding and play problems and, in this case, a great 'rest of the story' that occurred at the other table. Try not to read ahead until you have formulated your answer to the posed question.

Again, 3◊ ends the auction – and 3NT is a disaster. Everyone should agree that Double is the correct call. Considering the first double, would your partner interpret this as penalty or take-out?

My LHO passed and Matilda hissed, '2♠'. What a revolting development. But there is always an escape to 3◊. What do you bid now?

West	North	East	South
NB	NB	2◊	Dbl
2♡	NB	NB	Dbl
NB	2♠	NB	?

Consider that partner must be short in hearts and somebody has to have some diamonds. But also consider the background. Matilda's nastiness has bordered on unethical behaviour, so I thought I might teach her a lesson by overbidding. I bid 5◊. The volume of the expected double on my left was even louder than I expected. I elected not to redouble. The lead, as expected, was the ♡K.

♠ Q J x x
♡ x
◊ 7 6 x x
♣ J x x x

```
      N
  W       E
      S
```

♠ A K
♡ A J 10 x x
◊ A K 10 9 8
♣ x

Matilda slams down her cards daring you to make the contract on the left.

You quietly inspect the dummy ignoring Matilda's glare. Turning to LHO you ask an important question on bidding style, and you are reassured: their Flannery bid promised exactly 5 hearts and 4 spades.

Can you make the contract?

The play illustrates simple, but proper technique in trick-taking. Win the lead with the ♡A. Test the diamonds by playing the ◊A, getting the bad news as East discards a heart. Unblock the ♠A–K, then ruff a heart. Play the ♠Q, discarding your club. Then cross-ruff the hand letting West win with his ◊Q–J at his leisure (overruffing, though, if West ruffs low). You have made 5◊ doubled vulnerable, and Matilda is beaming with pride. You score plus 750, vulnerable against non-vulnerable opponents.

Can you guess how many IMPs are won or lost as a result of comparing your score with that achieved by your team-mates?

157

The incredible answer to how many IMPs you won or lost when you make 5◊ doubled vulnerable *vs* non-vulnerable opponents is *minus* 16 IMPs! This was the full deal:

```
Dealer: West              ♠ Q J x x
N/S Vul                   ♡ x
                          ◊ 7 6 x x
                          ♣ J x x x
         ♠ x x x        ┌─────────┐      ♠ x x x x
         ♡ K x          │    N    │      ♡ Q x x x x
         ◊ Q J x x      │ W     E │      ◊ –
         ♣ K x x x      │    S    │      ♣ A Q 10 x
                        └─────────┘
                          ♠ A K
                          ♡ A J 10 x x
                          ◊ A K 10 9 8
                          ♣ x
```

At the other table the bidding started out the same. East opened a Flannery 2◊ on his moth-eaten 8-count, and South doubled. But now something went terribly wrong: West, with his ◊Q–J–x–x, redoubled – and all passed! This contract went down *five* for minus 2200. The defence didn't play as well as I did, since it is possible to take the contract six off.

In case you are wondering – we still won the match. I had to play one more round with Matilda the Hun. We decided not to defend our title.

UNFAIR DEFENCE

A beginner who had just gone down in a 3NT contract shook his head sorrowfully: 'I would have made that contract', he said, 'if the defence hadn't ruffed in!'

(from Double Talk, the West Devon CBA newsletter)

COMMON-SENSE SIGNALS

BY DAVID BARNES

Opinion is divided three ways over what is most important to show partner when discarding, with votes going to:

(1) Encouraging or discouraging in the suit discarded;
(2) Preference for some other suit;
(3) Length in the suit discarded.

Each method has its merits and will work well on some hands. I'm sure that the debate will continue for many years.

One hears much less about what to do when following suit as defender. There is still an argument for suit preference, but often one is short in declarer's suit and the message is not clear to partner, because declarer can have several cards concealed. This leads to many partnerships opting for signalling length on declarer's (or partner's) lead, leaving poor partner to work out the whereabouts of Aces and Kings.

Whatever your chosen method, it has to be tempered with common sense – and above all, don't commit the cardinal sin of signalling with a winning card! If your agreed signalling methods call for the play of a high card, common sense will normally warn you not to be over-zealous. Holding 8–6–4–2 play the 6, unless you can see from dummy that you can afford to play the 8. It is surprising how often the fourth round of a suit is won by the 8 – but only if you haven't played it already to signal length!

Similarly, if you hold three cards in a suit, and you have agreed to show length by playing low to indicate an odd number, only do so when you don't need to force a high card from the next hand. Look at this deal (printed overleaf) from a seven-board Swiss Teams match:

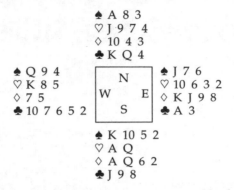

♠ A 8 3
♡ J 9 7 4
◊ 10 4 3
♣ K Q 4

♠ Q 9 4   ♠ J 7 6
♡ K 8 5   ♡ 10 6 3 2
◊ 7 5   ◊ K J 9 8
♣ 10 7 6 5 2   ♣ A 3

♠ K 10 5 2
♡ A Q
◊ A Q 6 2
♣ J 9 8

It is difficult to stay out of the 26-point game, and both pairs played in 3NT. This contract does not look likely to make on a club lead, as West has an entry to clear the suit and another entry to enjoy it.

However, at the table against me, the defence were playing distributional signals, with a low card showing an odd number in that suit. I won the second club lead in dummy, and took the heart finesse. West led a third club to dummy's Queen, but, as you can see, after successfully finessing in diamonds, I was still a trick short and needed to turn to the spade suit. If West had started with ♠Q–7–4 I could have played low towards dummy, covering whatever West played and, if necessary, inserting the ♠10 on the way back. As it was, West could play the ♠9 on the first round of the suit, thus guaranteeing a trick for his ♠Q – but the spectre of Distributional Signals reared its ugly head. When I led the ♠2 from hand, West played the ♠4 – his lowest card – to signal length! The ♠8 from dummy drew East's ♠J, and now I could afford to win any return from East, cash the ♠A, cross back to my ♠K, without ever being in danger of West gaining the lead with the ♠Q – and with the added bonus of knowing that my fourth spade would be a winner. The 12-IMP swing on this hand was exactly the winning margin in the match.

FREAK SHOW

BY DAVE HUGGETT

It is annoying to misplay a hand at the best of times, but even more so when partner has taken a good view in the face of heavy pre-emption.

On this deal, South had opened 5◊ at Game All, to blot out the majors, and North had taken an enterprising view when he had raised to six. Declarer was lucky to find his partner with most of the right cards on this freak hand from a local league match – but how should he have played 6◊ on the ♡Q lead?

♠ A Q 6 3
♡ K 6 5 4
◊ A Q
♣ J 6 5

```
    N
W       E
    S
```

♠ 2
♡ –
◊ K J 10 8 7 6 4 2
♣ A Q 9 3

Solution on page 218.

PARTNERSHIP'S AGREEMENT

Whilst making very heavy weather of an easy contract, South caught North's eye. 'What's that grin for?' he asked.
   'It's not a grin', replied North. 'It's a sneer!'

RUSTY CHARLIE LEARNS BARON

BY DUMMY RUNYON (ALIAS SAM JONES)

Sitting discussing the merits of the Baron 3♣ Convention with Three Fingers Louie over a quiet dark rum in Mindy's, prior to the first heat of the Broadway Pairs, I am abruptly disturbed by a large hand on my shoulder – and the unmistakable gravel voice of Rusty Charlie.

'Now if I have any idea Rusty Charlie is coming my way, you can go and bet all the coffee in Java I will be somewhere else at once, for Rusty Charlie is not a guy I wish to have any truck with whatever. In fact, I wish no part of him. Furthermore, nobody else in this town wishes to have any part of Rusty Charlie, for he is a hard guy indeed. In fact, there is no harder guy anywhere in the world. He is a big wide guy with two large hands and a great deal of very bad disposition, and he thinks nothing of knocking people down and stepping on their kissers if he feels like it.'*

'Hey! That sounds like a great convention! We'll give it a try tonight.'

'Unfortunately', I reply in a matter-of-fact tone, 'Walter Winchester is my partner this evening. It is a long-standing arrangement.'

'Hey Scribe!' barks Rusty Charlie across the restaurant. 'Your partner and me are playing a new convention tonight for the first time – awright?'

Walter commences a polite protestation, but when Mr Rusty turns around and gives him the old cold stare, Walter wilts with, 'Sure,

---

*Quoted from *Blood Pressure*, a short story by Damon Runyon from the omnibus edition of *On Broadway*.

Charlie. Great idea. I was thinking about taking in a show.' He heads speedily towards the nearest exit and is gone.

It is not long before the competition gets under way – Rusty unnerving the pairs who come to our table, and their mistakes make up for his.

After two hours of torture, I hear Rusty Charlie open 2NT as South, and I look closely at my North hand:

♠ 2
♡ Q J 10 5
◇ 10 9 8 2
♣ J 10 5 3

```
      N
W         E
      S
```

♠ A K Q
♡ K 8 4 3 2
◇ Q J 4
♣ K Q

It's a borderline hand for 3NT, but an excellent opportunity for Baron, so I bid 3♣. Rusty replies *3NT!*

A spade is led, and Charlie wins in hand, then forces out the ♡A, wins the spade return and forces out the ♣A. He wins the third round of spades and cashes four hearts and three clubs for ten tricks, the opponents' ◇A and ◇K crashing together on the last trick.

'Three no-trumps plus one!' Rusty announces proudly, as I open the traveller to reveal an outright top, eight other players going one off in 4♡, losing the ♡A, the ◇A–K, and the ♣A.

'Why didn't you bid 3♡ over my 3♣?' I enquire.

Rusty rises slowly from the table and announces indignantly, 'Because the Baron Convention says to bid *four*-card suits! You shouldn't play conventions you don't understand!'

EAVESDROPPINGS

South: 'One No-trump.'
West: 'Two Clubs.'
North: 'Did you say Two Clubs?'
West: 'Yes.'
North: 'Oh, dear! That's messed me up completely!'

GOOD JUDGEMENT

BY RAYMOND BROCK

The Channel Trophy is a teams event, competed for annually by junior teams from Great Britain, France, Belgium, and the Netherlands. Each country fields both an Under-25s team and an Under-20s. In 1991 the event was excellently staged by the Dutch Bridge Federation in Cadzand, a small town just outside Zeebrugge.

The journey to Zeebrugge was remarkably uneventful. Much to the two captains' surprise, all members of both teams were at the pre-arranged meeting place when they arrived. However, the journey home was rather more eventful.

We were all booked on to a ferry out of Zeebrugge in the early evening, which unfortunately was scheduled to dock after the last London train was due to leave Dover. This meant than many players would have to spend the Sunday night in Dover. In addition to this, the weather was very windy, and it was feared that there might well be delays (or cancellations!). As it happened, play finished earlier than expected on the Sunday, and we asked the hotel to ring up and see if there was an earlier crossing. We were told that there was, and made arrangements with our hosts to arrive at Zeebrugge in time for the earlier boat. We were duly deposited by our hosts, only to discover that this earlier crossing no longer existed – yes, they knew that it appeared in their time-table, but it had been cancelled some while ago!

This left fourteen of us stuck in Zeebrugge for five hours on a Sunday evening – with no Belgian currency (since Cadzand was actually in the Netherlands, we only had Dutch currency!). We were not very far away from Ostend, so we decided to get a bus there, and hope for an earlier, shorter crossing – but in order to do this we first had to find some Belgian currency. We were told that there was a 'hole in the wall' money machine which accepted British cards, and off we all set. We did indeed find this machine, which did indeed take our cards, but while we were doing this a splinter group noticed that the station was nearby and went off to find out about trains. They came back to report that there was a train to Calais leaving in three minutes. A retrospectively foolish decision was made to take this train. The station did not take credit cards; we still had insufficient Belgian francs, but sterling was acceptable, so we had a quick whip around while the station master held up the train to give us time to buy our tickets.

This train turned out to be *very* slow! We had to change (and wait for a connection) once in Belgium (still with no currency, since we had used what we had as part-payment for the tickets) and once in France (where we had no currency at all). When we arrived in Calais we were in the centre of the town rather than the docks, and had to persuade a fleet of French taxi-drivers to take us to the docks for a pre-negotiated payment in *sterling*! And... of course, when we arrived at the docks we had just missed a ferry.

We did arrive in Dover before we would have done had we taken the later Zeebrugge crossing (by ten minutes), but were still too late for the last London train! However those ten minutes we saved were certainly not worth the effort involved – not to mention the cost. If you really try hard, you too can know what it is like to travel as part of the British Junior team!

CONTRADICTORY INSTRUCTIONS

At a Surrey 'No Fear' event, a player was heard to say: 'Why is the recommended lead from Ace-King doubleton the King? I've been taught never to underlead an Ace!'

(from the Surrey CBA Bulletin)

MAYDAY! MAYDAY!

BY ALASDAIR FORBES

Hell hath no fury like a man left to play in his own SOS redouble. What is an SOS Redouble, you may well be asking? In the Portland Cup (the main Mixed Pairs event in Great Britain), a few years ago this vivid example occurred on Board 26:

```
Dealer: East                ♠ 5 2
Game All                    ♡ Q J 10 9 4 3
                            ◇ K 2
                            ♣ K 10 6

        ♠ 8 7 3         ┌─────────┐       ♠ A 9 4
        ♡ 7 6           │    N    │       ♡ A 8 5 2
        ◇ J 8 7 5       │  W   E  │       ◇ A Q 9 6
        ♣ 8 7 4 2       │    S    │       ♣ J 5
                        └─────────┘
                            ♠ K Q J 10 6
                            ♡ K
                            ◇ 10 4 3
                            ♣ A Q 9 3
```

South	West	North	East
			1♡
Dbl	NB	NB	Redbl
End			

We would all open the bidding with the East cards, and 1♡ is fair enough. South had a reasonable take-out double, and West as good a pass as you will find. The textbook says that you should have four trump tricks to convert a one-level double to penalties, so North passed and awaited developments. East, who realized that his side was in trouble, now produced a redouble for rescue – a risky business, in view of the fact that the bid had not been discussed by the partnership. West sat for about two minutes, but could not bring herself to bid either 2♣ or 2◇, which is the best spot for East–West. She finally passed, as did North, and you have to lead as South.

The ♡K is the correct card, but South chose the ♠K. East won and led the ♣5 to South's ♣9, and North sensibly overtook in order to play trumps. She naturally played the ♡Q and declarer was delighted to see South's King fall under the Ace. Now East tried the ♣J, and South recovered from his earlier error by letting this run to North's ♣K. On the ♡J, ♡10, and ♡9, South discarded his losing diamonds – so by the time trumps had been cleared and he had been put back in hand with a club, he had only black-suit winners to cash, and East did not even score his ◊A.

HELL HATH NO FURY LIKE A MAN
LEFT TO PLAY IN HIS
OWN SOS
REDOUBLE

In fact, East was so upset that his opponents had to call the Director to convince him that the score for five down vulnerable, doubled and redoubled, is indeed 2800 points!

HAPPY ACCIDENTS

BY ALAN GRACE

The following hand was dealt in a recent club duplicate, and produced an excellent result because of a series of happy accidents:

```
         ♠ A K 9 4 3      ┌─────────┐      ♠ J 8 6 2
         ♡ –              │    N    │      ♡ 10 7 4 3
         ◊ A J 8 3        │ W     E │      ◊ 10
         ♣ K J 4 2        │    S    │      ♣ A Q 10 8
                          └─────────┘
```

I dealt the East hand and, after two passes, partner opened 1♠. North bid 2♡ and I raised to 3♠ – I can find no-one who supports this bid, everyone to whom I have shown the hand having contented themselves with 2♠. However, I relied on the Losing Trick Count, and because I could read partner either for a five-card suit or for 15+ points (we were playing a 12–14 no-trump, and he would have opened 1NT with a 4–3–3–3 or 4–4–3–2 hand and fewer than 15 points), I decided that 3♠ was the most descriptive bid I could make.

Clearly partner thought that my hand was stronger than it was, for he launched into Blackwood, and bid a reluctant 6♠ after learning of my one Ace and no Kings.

The ♡A was led, and I tabled dummy with the thought to partner that if dummy isn't as strong as you expected you just have to play the hand well – and this is what he proceeded to do. The heart lead was ruffed, the ◊A cashed and followed by a diamond ruff, heart ruff, diamond ruff, a club to the King and a ruff of the last diamond. Clearly it is now best to play off the ♠A–K and then to play on clubs. If spades are not 2–2 (in which case you will make an overtrick), this play will succeed as long as the trumps are not 4–0. In fact partner elected to play on clubs, and was lucky when the ruff came from North, who held the guarded Queen. He was now still able to ruff the heart lead, draw trumps in two rounds, and make the remaining clubs.

Since, with the spade position as it was, we could not make more than twelve tricks, I can only conclude that the luck was with us.

COMPUTER-SCORED PAIRS

BY TONY HAWORTH

Most of us know the basic principles of match-pointed pairs scoring: a pair gets two points for each other pair they beat, and one point for each other pair that has exactly the same score as them.

Given this basic definition, how is it that sometimes, when results are posted, pairs end up with a total which contains a decimal point (e.g. 176.4)? This may have been due to multiplying a pair's actual score by a *factor*, to take into account the fact that they may have played fewer boards than other pairs; however, traditionally this would have been rounded up. More likely, if the results have been computer-scored, the computer program (if it is a quality one) will have applied a little-known formula to the results to take into account varying tops on boards.

The requirements for this can be appreciated by considering a six-table Mitchell movement, on which the board-top is 10. However, if a relay Mitchell is used, and the movement is not completed, some boards will only have a top of 8. Now, is it right that a pair who have a top on the first type of board should have the same 100% score as a pair who have a top on the second-type board (one pair has beaten five other pairs, and the other has beaten only four)? There is a finite chance that, if a board of the second type had been played one more time, the actual top may have been beaten

Mathematically the answer to this is no, and merely adding on a factor to a pair's overall score does not correct the situation. Computer-scoring can correct for this inconsistency by effectively bringing all boards to the same common top. In practice the formula is applied only to boards having a top of less than the maximum top in the event. The formula, which is applied to each score on the board, can be found in the Tournament Director's yellow book:

$$t = \frac{(m \times e) + (e - a)}{a}$$

where

t = the factored match-points to be awarded on the board to a specific pair.

m = the match points that would have been awarded to the pair based on the original top.

e = the maximum number of scores on any board in the event.

a = the actual number of scores on this board.

Applying this to a pair who had 8 out of 8 in the previous scenario results in the pair getting an equivalent 9.8 out of 10 (m = 8, e = 6, a = 5). Similarly, a pair who had 2 out of 8 now gets 2.6 out of 10 (scores are rounded to one decimal place, with 0.05 moving towards average).

More importantly, the same formula should be applied to scoring multi-session events. For example, in the club pairs championship the board-top in the first week of 'we can beat anyone else' enthusiasm (when fifteen tables turned up) will be 28. However, in the second week when the stark reality hits the club rabbits, and perhaps only nine tables turn up, the board-top will be 16. It is wrong merely to add the percentages for the two weeks, even though the same number of boards have been played in each session. The above formula should be applied to each board for the second week, whereby all the boards will appear to have a common top of 28 (for example, a pair getting 6 out of 16 will score 10.7 out of 28).

Now, before all the club treasurers shudder at the thought of increased payments to scorers, I would emphasize that this procedure only applies when computing facilities are available. For manual scoring, it is accepted that the overall factoring of results is perfectly adequate.

A BEGINNER'S PROBLEM

BY ALEC SALISBURY

Lack of experience often leads beginners to bring many questions to their bridge teacher, who tends to establish typical answers that can be recalled instantly. The question which I am most frequently asked is, 'Is it wrong to lead from an A–Q holding?'

A lot of the time this lead is unattractive for an obvious reason — declarer may have the trappable King. However, holding five or more cards in the suit, this can be an effective lead against a no-trump contract. Take a favourite example.

West is on lead with this hand after this bidding:

♠ 6 5		*South*	*North*
♡ 9 8		1♡	1♠
◊ A Q 9 6 2		3NT	End
♣ Q J 10 7			

The ♣Q looks safe, but it is not aggressive enough and can only hope to establish one trick, or at best two, for the defence. Moreover, two further entries are needed to establish and enjoy the suit. The ◊6 (fourth highest) is better. Sure, it probably gives up a trick to declarer's ◊K, but the suit could reel in four tricks for the defence. Consider the following example:

Dealer: South
Love All

	♠ A Q 9 8 2
	♡ Q 7
	◊ 8 4 3
	♣ 6 5 2

♠ 6 5		♠ K 7 4 3
♡ 9 8	N	♡ J 10 5 3
◊ A Q 9 6 2	W E	◊ 7 5
♣ Q J 10 7	S	♣ 9 4 3

	♠ J 10
	♡ A K 6 4 2
	◊ K J 10
	♣ A K 8

Even in this bad-case scenario, when declarer holds all the other three diamond honours, the ◇6 defeats the contract when East returns a second diamond after the spade finesse fails for declarer.

A TALE OF TWO EXPERTS

Two experts sat down for the final of the Consolation Pairs.

'The women in this room are not as pretty as the women in the other room', said one.

'If you hadn't played so badly', replied the other, 'we wouldn't be in this room!'

David Barnes

ACOL BIDDING QUIZ
BY AMANDA HAWTHORN

How would you bid the following hands? The bidding assumes rubber bridge or teams-of-four, and 'No Fear' Acol (only Stayman and Blackwood are allowed).

Deal 1:

Dealer: East
N/S Vul.

♠ 7 6 5 4 3	**N**	♠ A K Q 10 9
♡ 3		♡ 7 6 5
◇ Q J 10 9 8	**W** **E**	◇ K 6
♣ K 7	**S**	♣ 9 6 4

Deal 2:

Dealer: East
Game All

♠ 2	**N**	♠ K Q 9 6 5 2
♡ A K 8 6 3		♡ 4 2
◇ A K 9 7 5	**W** **E**	◇ Q J 4 3
♣ K 9	**S**	♣ A

Deal 3:

Dealer: West
Game All

♠ A Q J	**N**	♠ 5 4 2
♡ A 10 5		♡ K J 8
◇ Q J 8 6	**W** **E**	◇ K 10 9 2
♣ A 8 5	**S**	♣ Q J 10

Solutions on page 219.

BIDDING SYSTEMS

Overheard at a National Ladies' Pairs event:
   'How did you bid board 24?'
   'Badly!'

A HIGH-LEVEL CONTRACT

BY ARTHUR PERELMAN

Dealer: South
N/S Vul

```
                    ♠ A 8 6 2
                    ♡ K Q 10 6 5
                    ◊ 4 3
                    ♣ K 4
    ♠ K 9 3          ┌─────────┐       ♠ Q 10 5 4
    ♡ 2              │    N    │       ♡ J 9 8
    ◊ Q J 5 2        │ W     E │       ◊ 10 9 8
    ♣ A J 10 3 2     │    S    │       ♣ Q 6 5
                     └─────────┘
                    ♠ J 7
                    ♡ A 7 4 3
                    ◊ A K 7 6
                    ♣ 9 8 7
```

South	West	North	East
NB	1♣	Dbl	2♣
4♡	5♣	5♡	End

In a recent match, I was South. West led a trump, East played the ♡9, and I won with my Ace. On the bidding, I had good hopes for the ♣K; so, if the trumps split 2–2, I would be able to ruff two spades for eleven tricks.

Hopefully, I played a second heart to the King, but West showed out. Now, my prospects looked poor. At any rate, I had to keep East out of the lead, so as to avoid a third round of trumps.

I led a small spade from dummy, and held my breath; East played low, and my Jack lost to West's King. So far, so good. I won the diamond return and led a club. West rose with his Ace.

After that, it was easy. Luckily, East had four spades and I could cross-ruff my way to eleven tricks.

When we compared results, I found that our opponents had played the hand in 4♡ just made; so, we had gained one IMP.

I turned to my partner: 'I was terrified that East would win the first round of spades and draw a third round of trumps.'

My partner sighed. 'The whole hand was a combination of errors. First of all, I don't like East's bid of 2♣. With only three clubs and a flat hand, she should pass. Your bid of 4♡ is even worse. You cannot be sure that I have hearts with you. There is no perfect bid on your hand – 3♡ or 3♣ are both possible. At least, they do not go past 3NT. When I heard your bid, I placed you with about six hearts, so I did not wish to defend. Hence my bid of 5♡.

'As for your play, that was not much better. You've just told me you were worried that East would win the first spade trick and lead a third trump. You should have tried harder to prevent this.'

YOU SHOULD HAVE MADE IT MORE DIFFICULT STILL!

'I thought I had made it difficult for her by leading from dummy.'

'You should have made it more difficult still.'

'How?'

'You should delay playing a second trump until you have lost one club and one spade. Even then, the defence might succeed, if West does not rise with his ♣A, so that East can get in twice – once with each of her black Queens – and draw trumps on each occasion. But that defence would be much more difficult.'

BRIDGE IS (NOT) AN EASY GAME

During a bridge class, a student who was trying to count a hand threw down her cards in desperation.

'It's no good', she said, 'if we were meant to play bridge we'd have been given thirteen fingers!'

Stephen Cashmore

WHERE ANCIENT MEETS MODERN

BY ERWIN SCHON(

The following hand was played in this year's Seniors' Congress Pairs Championship:

Dealer: North
Love All

	♠ A J 10 8 3	
	♡ Q 4 2	
	◇ 9 4	
	♣ Q J 9	

♠ –		♠ K 9 2
♡ K J 8 5 3	N	♡ A 10 9 6
◇ K 7 6 5 3	W E	◇ A Q J
♣ K 6 2	S	♣ 10 8 3

	♠ Q 7 6 5 4	
	♡ 7	
	◇ 10 8 2	
	♣ A 7 5 4	

North, who must have read Jon Baldursson's 1992 Bols Tip ('Bid at the first opportunity'), opened 1♠. East doubled for take-out, and South pre-empted with 4♠. West rather liked his hand, and tried 5♡. North decided he was worth a bid of 5♠, and, when East raised to 6♡, South – mindful of his ♣A – doubled.

North led the ♣Q and South won with the Ace to return another club. West won with the King, finessed the ♡10, then drew trumps in three rounds, cashed three master diamonds, and returned to hand with a spade ruff. He now continued with diamonds, discarding one club and one spade from dummy. The losing club was ruffed with dummy's last trump, and declarer was left with the thirteenth trump in his hand.

This hand brings out Simon's ancient principle, 'When in doubt, bid one more'. Had South gone to 6♠, his side would have lost 800 (four off doubled), whilst 6♡ would have cost 980 – which became 1210 thanks to the double.

Naturally North–South were booked for a bad score once they had driven East–West into a slam. However, this sort of thing is bound to happen in the modern aggressive game – even at a Seniors' Congress! I must say that I have a lot of sympathy with South, whose only fault was trying too hard for a top. Mind you, his double, and his disappointment when 6♡ made, showed a sad lack of familiarity with both ancient and modern bridge literature: had he read Simon's books he would have bid 6♠; and had he read Baldursson's tip, he would have known that with an aggressive bidding style you gain more than you lose – but that when you lose, you must just 'smile, and bide your time!'

AN IMPOSSIBLE CONTRACT

Declarer took twenty-five minutes to go down in 3NT.

'Could I have made it?' she enquired of partner as the Director hurried them to the next table.

'No way!' was the reply. 'You didn't have enough time!'

SOUVENIR FROM WALES

BY DAVID HAMILTON

The most satisfying and enjoyable deal to watch is one where declarer and defenders are equally brilliant, and the outcome of the cut and thrust is in the balance to the last few cards. Such a deal was seen on Vu-graph in a Camrose match between Wales and England:

Dealer: South
Love All

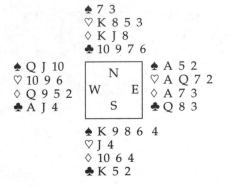

Chris Dixon in the North seat for England led the ♣7 against 3NT by West, and declarer played low in dummy, South winning with the ♣K. The spade return went to dummy's ♠A when declarer overtook his ♠J to preserve an entry to his hand. The ◊A followed, then a low diamond went to the ◊Q and North's ◊K. North now played the ♡3, ducked in dummy, South's ♡J winning. A spade lost to declarer's ♠Q, and a low diamond to North's ◊J left the position as shown at the top of page 179.

Dealer: South
Love All

♠ —
♡ K 8 5
♢ —
♣ 10 9 7

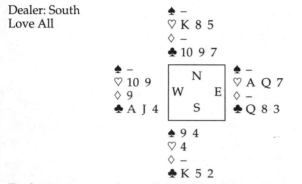

```
          ♠ —                         ♠ —
          ♡ 10 9      ┌─────────┐     ♡ A Q 7
          ♢ 9         │    N    │     ♢ —
          ♣ A J 4     │ W     E │     ♣ Q 8 3
                      │    S    │
                      └─────────┘
                    ♠ 9 4
                    ♡ 4
                    ♢ —
                    ♣ K 5 2
```

Declarer appears to have all the tricks at this stage, but Dixon had other ideas, and found the excellent play of the ♡K. The Welsh declarer, however, rose to the occasion by winning with the ♡A, finessing the ♣J, and playing the ♢9. North was forced to bare the ♣10, which was pinned when declarer went to dummy with the ♡Q and led the ♣Q. The lowly ♣8 provided the ninth trick for the contract.

Another match between Wales and England was looking to be disastrous for the spectators, when 72% of the deals were part-scores. It was not until hand 89 out of a total of 96 boards that the Vu-graph audience got some real excitement. This was the deal:

Dealer: West
Love All

♠ 10 8
♡ 6 4 3
♢ Q 7 2
♣ K Q 10 9 8

```
      ♠ K Q J 6 3 2                    ♠ A
      ♡ 8 2          ┌─────────┐       ♡ A K Q J 9 5
      ♢ 10 6         │    N    │       ♢ A 9 8 3
      ♣ A 7 6        │ W     E │       ♣ 3 2
                     │    S    │
                     └─────────┘
                   ♠ 9 7 5 4
                   ♡ 10 7
                   ♢ K J 5 4
                   ♣ J 5 4
```

The result came down from the Open Room that the Welsh pair sitting East–West had bid as follows:

West	East
1♠	3♡
3♠	4◊
4♠	4NT
5◊	5NT
6◊	7♠

On a club lead from North, declarer crossed to the ♠A and his problems were over when South showed out on the third round of hearts. He could ruff, draw trumps, and claim.

On Vu-graph the English pair had a different sequence:

West	East
1♠	3♡
3♠	4◊
4♡	4NT
5◊	5NT
6◊	6♡

The audience held their breath as South considered a lead. Eventually a club emerged, and that was a swing of 17 IMPs.

England won the match 11–7, but had this board been flat, they would also have won the Camrose Trophy which that year went to Scotland.

REBIDDING AT THE MINIMUM LEVEL

North–South play standard Acol, and thus can open the bidding on a four-card major. The bidding goes:

North	East	South	West
1♠	NB	NB	1♡

The Director is called, and the bid is accepted by North – who now bids 1♠. South alerts and, when asked, states that his partner has a five-card spade suit since he has rebid it!

Ron Heath

BIG HANDS

BY PAT HUSBAND

We have all experienced the pleasure of picking up our thirteen cards and sorting them into a blockbuster (where we fear partner cannot have much to contribute) or into an attractively-strong hand where we hope partner will collaborate with us in a slam investigation. Unfortunately, this doesn't happen many times in any playing session, so we don't get as much practice bidding big hands as we would like. Here is a way of organizing some concentrated practice and, of course, it is always enjoyable experimenting with big hands. If you have been taught by an EBUTA teacher, you may well know this method.

From your pack of cards, take out all the 2s, 3s, 4s, and the ♣5 (thirteen cards). Deal the remaining thirty-nine cards into three hands – North, East, South. West languishes with the rubbish!

Start with you taking the North hand (as dealer) and your partner the South hand, and bid them (don't be tempted to look at each other's hands at this stage). Record your bidding sequence and final contract. Then take the East hand (as responder) in place of the North hand, bid and record. Finally have partner take the North hand (as responder), and bid and record again. It is true that you have seen the North hand, but the exercise is still valid because now the hand is bid by responder, and not by opener.

When you have completed all three combinations, lay the hands out so you can discuss (and, you hope, justify) your bids and final contracts.

The beauty of this exercise is that: (a) you have concentrated practice; (b) you start to understand your partner's big-hand bidding more clearly (and vice-versa); and (c) you improve your joint abilities to reach slams when they are available, and keep out of them when they are not.

Happy slamming!

THE BIG GAME

BY JEFF MORRIS

It had been a long day. We had driven to Blackpool pleasure beach, and the kids had ridden all the roller-coasters in sight – sometimes with a reluctant Dad in tow. Back to the club for the evening to organize the rubber bridge. Strangely enough, the last thing a bridge-club organizer wants to do is actually to play bridge: there are so many distractions – questions to answer, rulings to give, people to talk to, things to arrange – that to be sat playing bridge is definitely bad business.

However, there are times when there is no option but to make up, and mostly one can play on automatic pilot whilst keeping an eye on the rest of the room. But there is one game that requires your total concentration and attention – The Big Game.

The Big Game in Manchester is the highest-stake rubber bridge game played in the club. Unlike London, the high-stake game is only a modest £5 per hundred (compared with £150 to £200 per hundred), and it is a game that is always of an extremely high standard. The better players for miles around make a point of playing. Participating in The Big Game reminds me of the advice aspiring young players were often given: play rubber bridge for a stake where it hurts to lose, and you'll soon improve!

There is much to be learnt playing in this game. Particularly, your judgement in competitive situations is tested and developed because not only are the players all of top-class standard, but they also know each other's game intimately through years of playing together. Obviously, to sit in and play in the game without knowing the players puts you immediately at a disadvantage – but there are other less obvious factors which also put you at a disadvantage.

I had never heard of 'form' before I played rubber bridge. To be on good form means not only holding good cards, but that things will go well for you. And when you are in *bad* form, not only do you have bad cards, but whenever you have a two-way decision to make you will always guess wrong – and when you are in what looks like a solid contract, the cards will break horrendously. If you are playing regularly in the game, you will know who is on form and who is not, and bid and play accordingly.

So, after a long day on the roller-coasters, and a long evening organizing the bridge club, came the call – at about 1.30 a.m. – to make up The Big Game. I sat down to a series of uneventful hands in which we managed to get vulnerable. Then I picked up the South hand below:

♠ 10 8 6 5
♡ A K 9 7 5 3
◇ 4
♣ Q 7

```
      N
  W       E
      S
```

♠ A K Q 9 3
♡ 10 4 2
◇ A Q 8 5
♣ A

After two passes, I opened 1♠. Partner responded with a jump to 3♡, which – since he was a passed hand – showed a four-card fit and a good five-card heart suit. I checked for Aces, decided not to be greedy, and settled for the small slam in spades. A club was led, which I won with my Ace.

I took stock. I was glad not to be in 7♠, which would require the heart suit to be played for no losers, but 6♠ seemed to be quite straightforward. I would draw trumps and then play on hearts to make five spades, five hearts, and two Aces for my contract. I played the ♠A – and the hand on my left discarded. A minor setback, I thought, because although the trumps were four-nil, I would be able to finesse the ♠J once I had got to dummy. How to get to dummy? Well, I could ruff a diamond and draw trumps, but if I had to lose a heart, a diamond could also be cashed against me. No, I would cross to dummy with the ♡A, finesse the spade, draw trumps, and duck a heart to make twelve tricks.

I led a heart to the Ace – and the hand on my right ruffed. This was not according to plan, and slowly realisation dawned on me that I had done something *very* silly. Of course, I should have allowed for the possibility of four hearts on my left by leading the ♡10 and, if it is not covered, running it. Right-Hand Opponent can ruff it, but whatever he returns I can draw his remaining two trumps, and then finesse the hearts for my contract.

I did misplay the hand, but it nevertheless was extremely unlucky to go down. After all, it did require two four-nil splits to defeat it. The cards did not forgive, and the opponents went on to win the rubber.

However, when I came to enter the score on the 'slogger', came the clue that I had missed: the opponent on my left had won every rubber that evening, and my partner was the biggest loser. With such information on the players' *form* I would have been alerted to the bad breaks from the word go!

A WEEK TO REMEMBER

BY MAX POWELL

On our way to Killarney, we stopped in Stourbridge where our friends Jean and Brian Standish invited my wife and me to play in the evening duplicate at the Stourbridge Bridge Club.

I played with Jean, who introduced me at each table and, to my embarrassment, extolled my supposed virtues – with the inevitable result that very polite opponents stayed out of unmakeable games that were bid at other tables. On the positive side, I was able to renew my acquaintance with some of the members whom I had met on bridge holidays or at congresses where I direct and they, without exception, expressed their surprise to see me playing. Why is it that Tournament Directors are not expected to enjoy the game themselves?

Eventually, we arrived at Table 13 to play Boards 13 and 14, and had this first-in-a-lifetime experience. Playing Acol, after three passes I opened 2♠ with the hand opposite and the bidding went:

West
♠ A K Q 7 4 2
♡ A
♢ A J 4 3
♣ 5

South	West	North	East
		NB	NB
NB	2♠	NB	3♣
NB	3♢	NB	4♢
NB	4NT	NB	5♢
NB	7♠	End	

Jean had shown a positive response, so now I wanted to know specifically if she had any support for diamonds, so I bid 3♢. When I heard the response of 4♢, wild horses were not going to hold me, but, inasmuch as we were not a regular partnership, I confirmed that Jean held the ♣A, then I bid the grand slam in spades.

The ♡K was led and dummy came down with:

East
♠ 10 9 8 6
♡ 8
♢ Q 10 2
♣ A 10 9 7 6

Having drawn the outstanding trumps, with no other course open even to Zia, I held my breath and led the ♢Q. This was promptly covered by the bare King, and the contract rolled home.

Then came Board 14:

♠ 7 6 5 4 3 2			♠ A K Q J 10 9 8
♡ 9	N		♡ A 10 8 7 6 5
◇ –	W E		◇ –
♣ 9 8 6 4 3 2	S		♣ –

First to bid, my partner opened 2♠ with the East hand above, and South overcalled 6◇. Having no defence, I bid 6♠ which Jean promptly converted to 7♠. South led the ◇A, and when dummy came down my partner claimed, stating that she was going to cross-ruff the hand.

Thus, for the first time in forty-five years of playing, two consecutive hands had occurred on which my partner and I had bid grand slams in the same suit! In addition, our overall 57.5% score was sufficient to win – certainly a night to remember!

Subsequently, my wife and I attended the 50th Killarney Congress which was held in the Lake Hotel. The Welsh contingent, knowing that when I run events I am rather a martinet as regards time, kept telling me I would have to relax and not look at my watch. They had really no need to worry: the hospitality of the Irish, combined with an excellent hotel, superb restaurant, and fantastic views over the lake and the mountains beyond soon rendered the wrist-watch an unnecessary burden.

So, instead of the advertised 7.45 p.m., the actual starting time could be anything up to 9.00 p.m. and no-one would be worried, everybody enjoying the extra drinking and socialising time. Certainly there was no time lost by calling the Tournament Director: in fact, I personally did not hear one call during the whole week we played there. The open pairs, in which the majority of the competitors played, was laid out for sections of twelve tables with pre-set travellers. Pairs moved up the tables and when eventually they were full, everyone started play, and then moved for each round, by general consensus – without any Tournament Director being involved.

During the week, bridge was only played in the evenings, which gave ample time for golf and sightseeing. The memories of watching dolphins frolic off Slea Head, the beautiful lakes of Killarney, and the wonderful views on the 'Ring of Kerry' will remain always with us.

SPOT THE JOKER

BY STUART JONES

I was playing South in a team-of-four match against a strong partnership. I knew that West was very accurate in both his bidding and play, whereas East, also a very good player, sometimes played with flair.

On the deal shown below, with no intervening bidding, we reached 6♡. Understandably, West chose to lead the ♡8 rather than a club, East contributing the ♡9. I won with the ♡10, and the ♡A at trick two confirmed the 3–1 break.

Dealer: South
E/W Vul.

```
                    ♠ A K Q 9 2
                    ♡ Q 5 2
                    ◇ Q J 5
                    ♣ 7 4
        ♠ J 10 4              ♠ 8 6 3
        ♡ J 8 3      N        ♡ 9
        ◇ K 10 7   W   E      ◇ 9 8 6 3 2
        ♣ A 9 5 2    S        ♣ K 8 6 3
                    ♠ 7 5
                    ♡ A K 10 7 6 4
                    ◇ A 4
                    ♣ Q J 10
```

So at tricks three and four I cashed the ♠A–K. West played first the ♠4, then the ♠10, while East contributed the ♠6 and ♠3. East–West play high-low to signal an even number of cards so that, when I called for the ♠Q at trick five and East played the ♠8, this card suggested that he also held the ♠J. But West had indicated an *odd* number of cards in the suit, and I trusted him to be reliable.

Playing East as the Joker, I discarded the ♣Q from hand, drew the last trump with dummy's ♡Q, and discarded two more clubs on the master spades, eventually conceding a diamond trick at the end.

East smiled at his partner and apologized for his misleading signal – explaining that he had hoped it might mislead declarer. Mind you, the Joker still had the last laugh, because they went on to win the match!

A MATTER OF CONCENTRATION

Declarer, trying very hard to make a difficult contract, turns to RHO asking for discard system. RHO refuses to answer.

An obnoxious player? No. The discard was from dummy!

Peggy Griffin

LOSING HEART

BY MALCOLM SIMPSON

Dealer: West
Love All

```
                          ♠ J 10
                          ♡ 5 4
                          ◇ Q 8 4 2
                          ♣ Q 9 6 3 2
        ♠ 9 7 6 2                        ♠ A 8 4
        ♡ A K Q J 10 2    ┌─────────┐    ♡ 8 7 6 3
        ◇ A              N │         │    ◇ 10 9 7 6 3
        ♣ J 7          W │    │  E   │    ♣ 10
                         │    S    │
                          ♠ K Q 5 3
                          ♡ 9
                          ◇ K J 5
                          ♣ A K 8 5 4
```

South	West	North	East
	1♡	NB	2♡
3♣	4♡	5♣	Dbl
End			

W hen you are defending a suit contract, you should never underlead an Ace!'

Dr Crowe glowered at me as he recorded yet another plus score:
'The good books say nothing about underleading A–K–Q–J–10. But
then they don't cater for chaps like you, who think they can get round
the boss by letting him win. It will do you no good, old fellow. My
senior managers are all born winners, not born losers!'

A few months ago it had seemed like a good idea to invite my boss
and his wife round for a weekly evening of rubber bridge. I had this
silly idea that it might have a belated influence on my career prospects.
But, after a few months, the reverse seemed to be the case. Dr Crowe
seemed to lead a charmed life, especially at the bridge table, while I
always take the losing finesse or make the phantom sacrifice.

After a competitive auction to 5♣, my wife judged correctly (for
once!) that we had three potential losers in 5♡, and doubled Mrs
Crowe's final bid. My opening lead of the ◇A was obvious, but what
should I lead next to ensure three tricks? My wife must have some

expectation of a defensive trick to have doubled, but how was I to know that she had the ♠A? She had supported hearts on the first round of bidding. I have never known her to do this without at least four, so Dr Crowe had one heart at most.

With some likelihood that I was about to impress my boss in no uncertain manner, I selected the ♡2 for my next lead. All my wife had to do was to win the trick with the ♡9 and give me a diamond ruff. If she had the ♡9, that is. What actually happened was that Dr Crowe took the second trick, and conceded just the ◊A and the ♠A for his contract.

'How do you feel about an early retirement?' asked Dr Crowe.

'Sounds a great idea!' I replied, believing that at last my long and undistinguished career was about to come to a most welcome end. 'I wonder just how much money I am entitled to?'

Dr Crowe looked a little indignant.

'Well, according to me, it's we who are entitled to £4.20. We did agree 10p a hundred, so I would be glad if you would settle up, so that I can get an early night. I am flying to the States tomorrow, along with my deputy, and leaving you at the helm. And for some strange reason I feel a bout of insomnia coming on!'

EASY AFTER ONE CLUB

BY RICHARD KENT

To bid or not to bid – that is the question. So the Prince of Denmark's bridge-playing cousin, Slamlet, mused – thus raising one of the fundamental philosophical problems that has plagued bridge-kind ever since.

Playing in the Casino De Cartagena open Torneo De Bridge in Spain in early May with Alan Phillips, a former Scottish Singles Champion, I pulled the following hand out of the board:

♠ 10 5
♡ 10 7 6 5 2
◊ 10 8 7 3
♣ A 10

Alan opened 1♣ (playing five-card majors, plus five-card diamonds with a strong no-trump). We don't demand a negative on a bust, even though the bid may be made on a singleton, so I could have passed, but I decided that my Ace and four Tens just about justified a response of 1♡. I immediately regretted my decision when he now bid 2♡ – unconditionally forcing for one round. After a lot of thought, I settled for the least strength-showing bid, 3♡, confirming a five-card suit and hoping that partner would not get over-excited. My worst fears were realized when he pulled the 'stop' card out of his bidding box, and slapped down the 6♡ card immediately after it. Everybody passed, Left-Hand Opponent led the ◇A, and dummy went down with:

♠ A K Q
♡ A K J 4
◇ 5
♣ K J 9 7 2

This was much better than I deserved! I took the spade switch on the table, and the hand presented no problems, as the trumps broke 2–2, two losing diamonds were ruffed, and one went on dummy's third spade. Even the ♣Q was doubleton with LHO, so I would have made seven on any other lead. Isn't it strange how everything is always right when you don't need it?

My outrageous good fortune was revealed fully when we opened the traveller and discovered that we were the only pair to have bid the slam – although, of course, everybody had made twelve tricks.

I was asked afterwards by another pair how we had managed to find the slam. They had, they said, opened with an Acol 2♣ bid, but had subsided in 4♡ and wanted to know how we had managed to get beyond game. 'Ah!' I said. 'My partner reckoned that he wasn't strong enough for a 2♣ opening with only 21 points – and, after 1♣, it's easy!'

EAVESDROPPINGS

'How could you possibly make that contract?'
'I had the right opponents!'

Maureen Dawson

THE PROFESSIONAL

BY JIM MULCAHY

My involvement in bridge started several years ago, when – for my sins – I taught bridge at Adult Education classes.

After some years, I decided to expand my hobby and opened the Bromley Bridge Club. With over two hundred and fifty members, and fifteen to twenty-plus tables, three times a week, this is now a thriving, friendly club. We moved to new premises about two years ago, and have fitted air conditioning so that we do not have any problems with the anti-smoking brigade. One of the things I like best is *not* interfering in other people's business and enjoyment. We can now provide an atmosphere that is very friendly, and a good-quality game. Hosts are available two evenings a week. Table money is kept to a minimum (£1.25 per head), to include bridge, tea or coffee, and biscuits. Our only problem consists of two gentlemen, both endowed with deep, carrying voices – who often provoke other pairs, three or four tables away, to help them with their bidding. I wonder if they need it?

The worst part of running a club is the directing. Absolutely no-one listens to a word you say about the movement, cards, boards, etc., and often the players will decide to agree amongst themselves about the action they should take after an infraction. This is acceptable as long as there are no afterthoughts on anyone's part – then, look out for sparks. I will never forget the time they agreed to transfer two tricks after a revoke, and the only tricks left were taken with the A–K–Q of trumps. That round finished nearly ten minutes late, after much discussion and the formation of an appeals committee – something we had never needed before.

I am acquiring a fine collection of foreign coins. When the holiday season starts, it is amazing how many find their way into the table-money box. Only once have I made a profit – someone put a five-franc coin for a ten-pence piece, not too bad as it had a value of nearly 50p. Then again, someone once put in one of the old, twelve-sided three-penny pieces instead of a £1 coin. What a pity they don't have any real value! Still, I am never short of small change when I go on holiday or trips abroad.

A PROBLEM FOR IMPROVERS

BY MIKE WHITTAKER

How should South play ♠6 on the lead of the ♡K from North?

♠ A J 10 9 4
♡ J 7
◊ J 7 4 2
♣ 9 8

```
      N
 W        E
      S
```

♠ K Q 9 8 7 5 2
♡ A
◊ A K 5
♣ A Q

Solution on page 220.

(CLOSE) EAVESDROPPINGS

Whilst North was entering a top in the score-sheet for the 3NT contract which she had just made, West was busy pointing out to his partner the shortcomings of her defence. When the harangue progressed from a detailed analysis of the hand just played to East's defensive deficiencies in general, North intervened.

'I always thought my partner could be mightily unpleasant', she mused, 'but now I can see that I owe him an apology!'

Andrew Parker

COUNTING TRICKS

BY ALBERT DORRINGTON

How do we count the number of playing tricks a hand is expected to make? Quite a lot of bids are based on being able to do just that. For example, an Acol Two bid requires eight playing tricks; similarly, over-calls and pre-emptive bids are partly determined by the 'Rule of Two and Three' which, in turn, depends on being able to assess the trick-taking potential of the hand.

In my book *Bidding for Social Players* I devised the following method:

A–K–Q = 3
A–K = 2
A = 1
K = ½ (not singleton King)
Q = ½ if a higher honour is held in the same suit
J = ½ if a higher honour is held in the same suit
10 = ½ if two higher honours are held in the same suit
½ for the fourth card in the suit
1 for each additional card after the fourth one in the suit
With six or more cards in the suit, add ½ to the total.

When a bid is made using the trick count, some care is needed in the subsequent bidding. The bid is made on playing strength, and the strength is concentrated in the trump suit. The bidder's partner must value his hand keeping in mind his own supporting role, and using a method of valuation which is complementary.

Assuming that the bidder will not bid a suit without two honours in the suit, the partner may count as follows:

Trump suit:

A = 1 ½
K = 1 ½
Q = 1
J = ½
10 = ½

Other suits:

Void = 1 ½
Singleton = 1   ⎤
Doubleton = ½   ⎦——— with sufficient trumps
Honour cards = as above

I have been using this method for about two years, and it appears to work quite well; if anything, it undervalues some hands.

It is particularly useful when overcalling, and in my book I have tried to give some precision to the subsequent bidding, avoiding the use of a kind of 'hope-for-the-best' version of Acol.

IN MID-CONGRESS

The attractive declarer who had just butchered a cold 4♠ contract fluttered her eye-lashes. 'I'm so sorry, but I got little sleep last night: I kept thinking of all the mistakes I'd made during yesterday's session.'

'I'm amazed you slept at all', commented her partner dryly.

CAPS IN BRIDGE

BY SVEND NOVRUP

Why is it that only few bridge federations count the caps of their national team players?

If you play soccer, table tennis, ice hockey, or any other sport, you can be certain that your federation keeps the relevant statistics. Every time you represent your country in an official match, they note it on your card, and if you are successful you will some day be honoured for your 50th or 100th cap[*]. Later, you will appear on the all-time top-ten list, and you, your federation, and your sport will all enjoy a considerable amount of publicity. Now, during a world championship of handball or ice hockey, a player has a cap for each match. In one year such players can gain up to twenty or thirty caps. Why should bridge caps be counted otherwise? It is not satisfactory just to say that so-and-so played in the 1988 Olympiad: maybe two pairs played almost all the time, while the third pair only played a little. Then two pairs should have lots of caps, and the third pair only a few.

I have traced the caps of the Danish national teams after World War II, from the Nordic Championships in 1947 to the Salsomaggiore Olympiad in 1992. The statistics involve all teams playing official matches recognized as such by the Danish Bridge Federation, i.e. all the official bilateral matches played in Nordic, Common Market, European, World and Olympic championships. Whenever a player has played just one half of a match in such an event, he has a cap. Playing in both halves of a match does not increase the number of caps: what matters is to have played in the match – just as a soccer player has a cap if he has been sent on the field at the last minute of the match.

Bridge players have one advantage over their counterparts engaged in other sports: they last longer! The table-tennis player Claus Pedersen will never play in the national team again, as he is now in his forties. His total of 357 caps is probably final, and he will never overtake bridge players Stig Werdelin or Steen Møller, who are in their fifties but still

---

[*] So called because, in the early days of sports, the British men had to wear a special cap whenever they played in the national team – and so could count the number of appearances by the number of such caps. S.N.

active, with the possibility of improving their respective totals of 439 and 403 caps.

Bridge statistics have made headlines. Imagine the excitement when Werdelin was the first Danish sportsman to pass the 400-cap mark. And he is breaking his own record every time he sits at the table to represent Denmark. Kirsten Steen Møller is heading the list of caps in the Ladies Series with 191, ahead of Judy Norris with 147, but Norris has 60 more caps from the Open Series and thus is the woman player with most caps – 207. We do not count matches in Junior Teams: the age limits have varied too much, and the events have been of very different characters.

Apart from counting caps, bridge statistics can show how a nation has done against every other nation played over the years. For instance, we Danes fully appreciate the strength of American bridge, as against the USA we have only won once in seven matches, and lost the rest heavily. There are a lot of nations against whom we have never lost in up to five matches, whilst we did, in fact, lose once to many small countries – the Faroe Islands being one of them. That caused a national celebration in the North Atlantic in 1990, and is still the only victory for their national team. The nation we have played most is Sweden – but we do not like to discuss that much. Out of 121 matches we have won only 43, drawn 5, and lost 73!

Let us take a hand from a Danish league match featuring our record-holder Stig Werdelin. When he was once asked for a good hand he quoted this one, saying that he liked hands with a psychological point:

```
Dealer: South            ♠ K 6 2
N/S Vul.                 ♡ Q 4 3
                         ◇ K J 7 2
                         ♣ Q 5 4
       ♠ Q J 9 7 3    ┌──────────┐   ♠ 8 4
       ♡ J 6 5        │    N     │   ♡ K 10 8
       ◇ A 9 3        │ W     E  │   ◇ Q 8
       ♣ J 8          │    S     │   ♣ 10 9 7 6 3 2
                      └──────────┘
                         ♠ A 10 5
                         ♡ A 9 7 2
                         ◇ 10 6 5 4
                         ♣ A K
```

South	West	North	East
1NT	NB	3NT	End

West led the ♠Q to dummy's ♠K, and the problem was to lose the first diamond to West. Werdelin took a psychologically good line when he led the ◇2 off table at trick two. Who could blame East for ducking? When West ducked the ◇10, declarer was safe: a diamond to the King dropped the Queen, after which the contract could not be defeated.

A SIGNIFICANT DISCARD

South, declarer in 3NT, won the opening spade lead with the Ace, cashed the ♡A, and proceeded to rattle off dummy's seven-card solid club suit on which to discard her losing diamonds. On the third round of clubs, East discarded the ◇A.

'What is the meaning of this discard?' enquired declarer of West.

West thought for a while. 'I believe', he eventually replied, 'that he's telling me I led the wrong suit.'

POETIC JUSTICE

BY DAVID ELLIS

My mother and I were involved in an odd incident whilst playing in a recent No Fear pairs event in Chichester.

It was the last round of the afternoon, and we were running late, so there was a lot of noise and, even worse, everybody else seemed to be queuing up for tea right behind me. On the hand below I was North, declarer in 4♡. East led a club:

Dealer: West
Love All

```
                        ♠ K 3
                        ♡ A K 4 3
                        ◊ 2
                        ♣ Q 7 6 4 3 2
       ♠ 9 5                              ♠ A Q J 8 4 2
       ♡ Q 9 5          N                 ♡ 7 2
       ◊ K Q J 7 4    W   E               ◊ 10 9 5
       ♣ J 9 8          S                 ♣ 10 5
                        ♠ 10 7 6
                        ♡ J 10 8 6
                        ◊ A 8 6 3
                        ♣ A K
```

I cashed dummy's top clubs and then, after finessing against the ♡Q and drawing trumps, I ran the clubs discarding dummy's spades. Then I led a small spade and ruffed on the table. East played the ♠A and then led the ♠Q, which I won with my King.

Then, as we were discussing how many tricks I had made, I thought: 'That's funny. I thought I was going to make six, but I wasn't counting on making the ♠K.'

So I said: 'How many tricks did we make?' and East replied: 'Twelve. I made my ♠A.'

'But I ruffed it!' I cried.

This is what had happened: East, thinking that she had won the trick, had led out of turn to the last trick; I, by playing to the trick, had accepted the lead, so we made 4♡ plus three...

In other circumstances I would not have accepted the extra over-trick, but I felt it was poetic justice for the previous board but one, where the same player had been declarer in 5♣ and had made it after leading dummy's ♡K and playing the ♠J on it – and my mother, mistaking one black Jack for another, had played low from her ♡A-x-x holding!

One bungle, I felt, deserved another.

THE YARBOROUGH BOX

At most of my bridge classes I run a 'Yarborough Box'. Students contribute, usually 5p a session, and the proceeds go to the first person to hold a Yarborough. The money mounts each week, and I put a £5 limit on the award.

```
        ♠ –
  N     ♡ A K
W   E   ◇ A K Q J
  S     ♣ A K Q J 8 6 4

♠ 8 7 5 3
♡ 7 5
◇ 8 6
♣ 9 7 5 3 2
```

A few years back a husband and wife were opposing each other. The wife, sitting East, ended in 7♣ on the hand opposite. North held the ♣10, South (the husband) scored a trick with his ♣9, and the wife went one down.

Imagine her anger when the husband – adding insult to injury – claimed the £5 Yarborough prize!

Leslie Smith

BOB'S WIFE

BY JOHN BARR

The rain was teeming down as I made my way home round the M25. One minute the traffic was flowing smoothly, the next it came to a dead stop. My blood pressure was rising by the second as I anticipated my husband's reaction if I were to be late for the bridge match. Suddenly the traffic congestion eased, and I found myself alone in the fast lane. 'I might be home in time after all', I thought to myself as I checked my mirror, noting that the visibility was so affected by the rain and spray that I could only just make out the blue flashing light behind me.

'I'm sorry I'm late, darling. The meeting in Manchester was delayed, my plane was cancelled, the M25 was hell – and to top it all I got a speeding ticket'.

My explanation and apology fell on deaf ears. 'I've done your washing, your ironing, taken Jimmy to the doctor and Tiddles to the vet (or was it the other way round), hoovered your house, cleaned out your fishpond, taken lunch to your mother, and mended your computer. All you had to do was get home on time. Can't you get anything right? Why do I have to do everything?'

I was punch-drunk. My day had been dreadful, and I was trying to relax sufficiently to play a bridge match. The last thing I needed was an undeserved haranguing like this. 'Wait a minute', I said when some of Bob's comments had sunk in, 'what do you mean "mended your computer?" It's not broken.'

'Well, I didn't plan on telling you until after the match in case it

201

upset you – it just slipped out.' He paused. I have known Bob long enough to know that this was a 'dramatic effect' pause. My heart sank.

'You know the problem Tiddles has been having? Well...' He paused again. I felt sick. 'Well... I must have left your office door open (after I tidied, dusted and hoovered it) and Tiddles went to sleep on top of the monitor because it's so nice and warm...' I could guess the rest, but before I could berate Bob for letting the cat loose on my computer his voice-box had sprung into life again. 'But don't worry, it's all right now... at least, it's stopped belching black smoke, and the funny noise is more of a whine instead of sounding like your mother putting the car into reverse. Don't worry, let's play some bridge and you can relax.' When Bob says 'don't worry' twice in the same breath, I do worry. I knew I should have taken a back-up of the document I had spent all weekend writing. The last things I felt like doing were relaxing and playing bridge.

Bob thrust a convention card into my right hand, and a gin and tonic into my left hand, and led me through to the dining room where we were due to play the first set, which thankfully passed without incident. We were even 3 IMPs up at half time. Luckily for me, there was only one board of real interest in the whole match – it was towards the end of the second set:

♠ A 10 9
♡ 3
◇ A K Q J 7
♣ Q J 10 8

I opened 1◇, and the bidding continued around the table with 1♠, 2♣, 4♡. We were vulnerable and the opponents were not, so double was out of the question. Eventually I bid 4♠, Bob tried 5♡, and I signed off in 6♣. This was converted to 6◇, and I had to think again. The auction had been:

South	West	North	East
1◇	1♠	2♣	4♡
4♠	NB	5♡	NB
6♣	NB	6◇	NB
?			

Bob had followed a very strong sequence, but I did not feel I had a lot to spare for my bidding. I didn't want to round off the day by going one down in a grand slam, so I passed. Dummy was a disappointment:

Dealer: South
N/S Vul

```
              ♠ 8 5 2
              ♡ A Q
              ◇ 6 5 3 2
              ♣ A K 7 4
♠ K J 7 6 4 3   ┌─────────┐   ♠ Q
♡ –             │    N    │   ♡ K J 10 9 8 7 6 5 4 2
◇ 10 8 4        │ W     E │   ◇ 9
♣ 9 6 5 2       │    S    │   ♣ 3
                └─────────┘
              ♠ A 10 9
              ♡ 3
              ◇ A K Q J 7
              ♣ Q J 10 8
```

'Thank you, darling. I see you upgraded the hand because of the strong intermediate cards.' Bob looked perplexed – sarcasm is lost on him. The lead was a trump, which suggested that West had no hearts and was missing a spade honour, probably the Queen. I drew trumps and cashed the clubs, at which point I could place every card in the pack with some certainty. If I had guessed the position correctly, the outstanding cards were:

```
              ♠ 8 5 2
              ♡ A Q
              ◇ 6
              ♣ –
♠ K J 7 6 4 3   ┌─────────┐   ♠ Q
♡ –             │    N    │   ♡ K J 10 9 8
◇ –             │ W     E │   ◇ –
♣ –             │    S    │   ♣ –
                └─────────┘
              ♠ A 10 9
              ♡ 3
              ◇ J 7
              ♣ –
```

To this day I am not sure that I really knew what I was doing, but it seemed 'the right thing to do' – and it certainly worked. I exited with the ♠9. If West wins with the King (dropping East's Queen) he is endplayed, having to lead away from his Jack into my A–10. At the table West played the ♠J, and East was forced to win with the ♠Q and lead away from his ♡K to dummy's A–Q. As we took the cards from the next board the opponents muttered approving sounds, but Bob said only,

'I'm glad I decided to bid on. After all, the contract was solid, you didn't even have to take a finesse. Shouldn't you have tried a heart to the Queen for the overtrick?'

In the other room, North–South had somehow subsided in 3NT, making twelve tricks, and we won the match by 7 IMPs.

During the post-match drink, Bob spent half the time congratulating our team-mates for avoiding playing as badly as they usually do, and the rest of the time congratulating himself for bidding the 'solid' slam. As I eventually climbed into bed, exhausted, Bob was still talking about the slam hand: 'Why can't you ever do anything? I had to win the match single-handed.' A moment later, my head hit the pillow and I was asleep.

I awoke with a start at three in the morning. Bob was shaking me vigorously. 'Jimmy's crying', he said. 'Why don't you do something?' He was right. Jimmy's plaintive wails could be heard loud and clear on the baby alarm. Bob prodded me in the ribs. 'Do something', he intoned.

I leant over to the bedside table, switched off the baby alarm, and went back to sleep.

MEANS AND ENDS

BY TOM TOWNSEND

In a recent competition I benefited from one of the worst successful bidding sequences I have ever seen perpetrated by a competent partnership, or perhaps I should say a pair of competent partners.

♠ K 7 5
♡ A 10 5 3
◇ A K Q J 3
♣ Q

	N	
W		E
	S	

♠ A
♡ K Q J
◇ 9 6 4
♣ A K 8 6 5 2

Our team-mates' system discussion was something of a premonition, consisting of a Dutch auction starting with the pinnacles of each individual's knowledge of unnatural bidding, and ending with the highest common denominator, strong no-trump with most gadgetry left implicit.

They dealt with the hand above as follows:

South	North
1♣ (a)	1◇
1NT (b)	2♡ (c)
3♠ (d)	4◇ (e)
4♡ (f)	4NT (g)
6◇ (h)	7♡ (i)
End	
End	

(a) Natural or weak no-trump. A good honest start to the auction.

(b) South has a difficult bid here. Most players would choose from a straight-forward 3♣ and manufactured calls of 1♡ and 2♡. The bid of 1NT, showing 12–14 points balanced, was probably influenced by South mis-sorting his hand or forgetting his no-trump range, almost certainly both.

(c) An example of the implicit science mentioned above. North would pass over diamonds with a major in which to respond with a weak hand, therefore this 2♡ rebid is forcing.

(d) South has remembered what 1NT showed. Now get out of that! He adopts the principle 'when in doubt, make the lowest call which you are sure is forcing.'

(e) Having far too strong a stomach to object in principle to a splinter (shortage-showing bid) by a no-trump bidder, North continues with a cue-bid. His is not to wonder why.

(f) Difficult to know how much the extra values mitigate the lack of a fourth heart.

(g) Blackwood of some kind.

(h) Decides that the knowledge that his previous bidding has been thoroughly perverse will help partner much more than a control-showing response. And what odds against chancing upon the correct response?

(i) Inspired.

I have left our heroes anonymous, not because hearts broke 6–0 (because in fact all the breaks were kind), nor because of their modesty (neither feels shame at his action). Rather because I fear the publicity may cause them to be less often available to play with me in teams events.

For I am always told that only results count. And what could be better than achieving the best result possible on the current hand and shocking the opponents into future submission in the process?

EAVESDROPPINGS

At the end of the qualifying round for the EBU's National Women's Teams a notice went up with the details of the knock-out draw, all teams being referred to by their captain's name and initials.

'This can't be right', said one of the players, 'K.O. Losers are playing four matches!'

When it became clear that this was not intended as a joke, a kind lady took it upon herself to clear up the misunderstanding: 'You'll see the logic of it if you look at the results of the qualifying round', she gravely said. 'In Group B, "Bye" were thirteenth!'

THIRD AND LAST

BY RICHARD WHEEN

This double-dummy problem is rather different from those on pages 65 and 122 – and rather harder.

The contract is no-trumps and these are the remaining cards:

```
♠ -                    ♠ -
♡ A 3        N         ♡ K J 5
◇ K 9    W       E     ◇ 3
♣ 3 2        S         ♣ A Q
```

North–South hold between them:

```
♠ -
♡ Q 10 8 6 4 2
◇ Q J 8
♣ K J 6
```

Arrange the North–South cards between those hands in such a way that the *only* play to ensure that East–West make all six tricks on a double-dummy basis is for West (who is on lead) to begin by playing a small club to the ♣A, and for East then to continue by leading the ♡J.

Solution on page 220.

SOLUTIONS TO PUZZLES

Fearful Symmetry by Dave Huggett (page 11)

'We've missed it this time, partner', said declarer as soon as dummy went down, but he changed his tune when East showed out on the first round of trumps. 'Never mind, it's a good job I know all about elimination plays', he continued, as – with a bored air – he drew a second round of trumps, eliminated hearts and clubs, and cashed the Ace and King of diamonds. His diatribe quickly came to an end when East showed out on the second round of diamonds, for now there were two inescapable losers.

'Bad luck, partner', said North with heavy sarcasm. 'What a pity you did not cash just the ◇A before throwing West in with his trump. I think that makes it 100% guaranteed!'

The full hand was as shown:

```
                    ♠ A 8 7 6 2
                    ♡ A 7
                    ◇ K 9 6 2
                    ♣ K 2
    ♠ Q J 10      ┌─────────┐      ♠ –
    ♡ J 9 8       │    N    │      ♡ Q 10 5 4 3 2
    ◇ J 10 5 3    │ W     E │      ◇ 8
    ♣ Q 10 8      │    S    │      ♣ J 9 7 6 5 3
                  └─────────┘
                    ♠ K 9 5 4 3
                    ♡ K 6
                    ◇ A Q 7 4
                    ♣ A 4
```

A Miracle Chance by Ulrich Auhagen (page 25)

♠ J
♡ K 7 4 3 2
◊ A Q
♣ A Q 6 5 3

♠ A Q 6 5 4 3 2
♡ –
◊ K J 10 9
♣ K J

South has to hope that East has a 2–4–4–3 distribution, with the King of trumps on-side.

The play should go: heart ruff, ◊A, heart ruff, ◊Q, heart ruff, ♣J to ♣Q, heart ruff, ♣K to ♣A, club ruff, ◊K, ◊J ruffed with ♠J, playing a card from dummy at trick twelve to catch East's ♠K.

East might hold:

♠ K 9
♡ A 9 8 5
◊ 8 6 5 3
♣ 10 8 7

Tony's Play Problem by Tony Forrester (page 43)

♠ A K 3 2
♡ 4 3 2
◊ Q 5
♣ A K J 10

♠ 7 6
♡ A K Q J 10 9
◊ –
♣ 9 8 7 6 5

Play four rounds of trumps, discarding the ◊Q from dummy. Then play three rounds of clubs. The position (left) when the third club has been played is as below right:

♠ A K 3 2
♡ –
◊ –
♣ 10

```
      N
   W     E
      S
```

♠ 7 6
♡ 9
◊ –
♣ 9 8

If clubs are 4–0, the opponents must play either a diamond, in which case you ruff in hand and throw the ♣10 from dummy, or a spade, when you can cash a club, and then ruff a spade and cash the fifth club.

Crossword Puzzle by Don Putnam (pages 48–49)

Across: 1 Meanness; 5 Forced; 9 Jocosely; 10 Demons; 11 Reverses; 12 Phasma; 14 Astronomer; 18 Orotundity; 22 Re-echo; 23 Scrabble; 24 Creese; 25 Virtuoso; 26 Setter; 27 Intrigue.
Down: 1 Majors; 2 Alcove; 3 Nosers; 4 Silverside; 6 Open Hand; 7 Cross-imp; 8 Despairs; 13 Protection; 15 Four Aces; 16 Movement; 17 Duchesse; 19 Master; 20 Oblong; 21 Revoke.

The Guthrie Five by Nigel Guthrie (page 53)

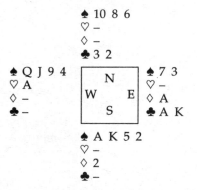

```
                ♠ 10 8 6
                ♡ –
                ◊ –
                ♣ 3 2
♠ Q J 9 4     ┌─────────┐     ♠ 7 3
♡ A           │    N    │     ♡ –
◊ –           │ W     E │     ◊ A
♣ –           │    S    │     ♣ A K
              └─────────┘
                ♠ A K 5 2
                ♡ –
                ◊ 2
                ♣ –
```

On a heart or small trump lead, win as cheaply as possible in dummy (playing a small trump from hand). Ruff a club with the ♠K, then lead a diamond to coup West.

However, there is a better defence…

If West leads the ♠Q, you win with your King. When you lead a diamond, West does best to discard, so you ruff in dummy with the ♠8. Now you run dummy's ♠10 to scoop East's ♠7. West is endplayed to lead from ♠9–4 into ♠A–5. Against this defence, the contract would fail if you swap the *three* and *five* of spades.

The First of Three by Richard Wheen (page 65)

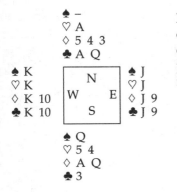

```
        ♠ -
        ♡ A
        ◊ 5 4 3
        ♣ A Q
♠ K              ♠ J
♡ K      N       ♡ J
◊ K 10  W   E    ◊ J 9
♣ K 10    S      ♣ J 9
        ♠ Q
        ♡ 5 4
        ◊ A Q
        ♣ 3
```

Play a diamond to the Ace and take the club finesse. Cash the other club honour, discarding the ◊Q. Ruff a diamond and play a trump to the ♡A. North's remaining diamond is good for the sixth trick.

Better than None by Dave Huggett (page 81)

After South decided to open 2♡ on his four-loser hand there was no way that North would be denied, and it was just a matter of time before they reached the small slam. West led the ♠K and declarer surveyed dummy bleakly, trying to conjure up a chance where none really existed. There might be, he felt, one tiny chance (which was better than none at all), and it depended upon East not knowing that declarer held a singleton spade. Accordingly, he won the opening lead and immediately played three rounds of clubs, giving the impression that he wanted to discard a losing spade. With the gods smiling, East ruffed the third club with the ♡3, but declarer overruffed and the trump Queen brought down the Ace and the King together. This was the full hand:

```
              ♠ A 7 3
              ♡ 8 7 6 4 2
              ◊ 3
              ♣ K Q J 8
♠ K Q J 9              ♠ 10 6 5 4 2
♡ K          N        ♡ A 3
◊ 10 8 6    W   E     ◊ 9 5 4 2
♣ 10 9 6 3 2   S      ♣ 7 5
              ♠ 8
              ♡ Q J 10 9 5
              ◊ A K Q J 7
              ♣ A 4
```

Polish Puzzle by Nigel Guthrie (page 98)

♠ A K Q J	N	♠ 10
♡ A 8		♡ K J 10 9
◊ A 8 7	W　E	◊ K Q 10 9
♣ A 8 7 6	S	♣ K Q 10 9

After a spade lead, cash the ♡K, ♣K, ◊Q–K–A. Then play three spades discarding three hearts, to leave:

♠ –	N	♠ –
♡ A		♡ –
◊ –	W　E	◊ 10
♣ A 8 7	S	♣ Q 10 9

Unless the ◊10 is good, discard it on the ♡A after North has played. Now:

A. If both opponents follow suit, then the opponent who is left clutching the ◊J can hold at most two clubs. Cash the top club on that opponent's left. If he discards, then finesse clubs into his hand.

B. If an opponent shows out on the ♡A – whether or not he discards the ◊J – then you know the exact distribution of spades, hearts, and diamonds; so you can deduce the club layout and play clubs accordingly.

For this exquisite *count squeeze* to work, the last squeeze card must be a *heart*, not a spade. You might say that you transfer the squeeze card from spades to hearts (by analogy with a transferred menace).

Crossword Puzzle by Roger Trowell (pages 106–107)

Across: 1 Hand of Glory; 9 Untruer; 10 Renew; 11 Pecan; 12 Ruction; 13 Everlastingly; 16 Elevens; 18 Raise; 20 Rolls; 21 Ice-cube; 22 Spade Guinea.
Down: 2 Aztec; 3 Diurnal; 4 Fire-resisting; 5 Lyric; 6 Ranking; 7 Purple Heart; 8 Twenty-seven; 14 Eye-flap; 15 Israeli; 17 Eased; 19 Inure.

Plan Your Defence by Bob Rowlands (page 109)

East's ♣3 should indicate a five-card suit (no need to signal to show the ♣A, therefore East gives count). West expects to win two club tricks and two diamond tricks, provided East has ◊Q–x–x or better, but if he continues clubs his partner may go wrong by playing a third club hoping for a trump promotion. A spade switch might cost if partner plays ♠K and declarer has ♠A–Q–9–8, so a passive trump is best.

The full deal:

```
                  ♠ J
                  ♡ A Q 9 6 2
                  ◊ 10 9 7
                  ♣ Q J 5 2
  ♠ 10 5 3 2      ┌──────────┐     ♠ K 7 6 4
  ♡ 10 4          │    N     │     ♡ 5
  ◊ A J 5 4 3     │ W     E  │     ◊ K Q 2
  ♣ K 4           │    S     │     ♣ A 10 9 8 3
                  └──────────┘
                  ♠ A Q 9 8
                  ♡ K J 8 7 3
                  ◊ 8 6
                  ♣ 7 6
```

Second Puzzle by Richard Wheen (page 122)

```
                  ♠ Q
                  ♡ Q J
                  ◊ Q J 7
                  ♣ –
  ♠ J             ┌──────────┐     ♠ K 4
  ♡ A 2           │    N     │     ♡ K 3
  ◊ 8 5 4         │ W     E  │     ◊ 10 6
  ♣ –             │    S     │     ♣ –
                  └──────────┘
                  ♠ A 2
                  ♡ –
                  ◊ 9 2
                  ♣ 3 2
```

215

North should lead a diamond honour, South playing ♢9. East and West do best to play low on this lead. North now leads a heart ruffed by South. Again, both East and West do best to play low. South now leads his remaining trump. If West discards a diamond on this, he will promote North's second diamond, so he will probably discard his heart or spade:

(a) If West discards his spade, so does North, and East must then discard his heart to avoid promoting South's second spade or allowing South to finesse West in diamonds. The lead of the ♠A then squeezes West who has to discard so as to allow North to win the rest of the tricks.

(b) If West instead discards his heart, North discards a spade, and East is squeezed instead. If he discards a spade, then South's second spade becomes good; if he discards his heart, then North's heart becomes good; and if he discards his diamond, it allows South to finesse West's diamond and make a second diamond trick. In any event, North–South make the remaining tricks.

Did You Scrape a Win? by Bernard Magee (page 136)

It appears that partner's ♡J is a singleton, and thus declarer has twelve tricks – six hearts, five spades, and the ♣A. If declarer does not hold the ♢A, then for his initial cue-bid he must surely hold both the ♣A and ♣K, otherwise he would have bid a direct 4♡. If declarer's hand is ♠x ♡ A K x x x x x ♢ K x x ♣ A K, he will be able to draw two rounds of hearts and discard all his diamonds on dummy's spades. Thus he's sure of twelve tricks…unless he has a spade void! Now there is no entry to dummy and the contract is in danger.

However, declarer can still give himself a chance by playing ♡A–K and putting you in hand with the ♡Q. With no clubs or hearts to return, you would then be obliged to lead a spade or a diamond – and the latter may well provide an entry to dummy.

There is only one solution: you must throw your ♡Q under the ♡K on the second round of trumps, and declarer is helpless. Of course I hope you remembered to throw the ♡6 under the Ace on the previous round of the suit, otherwise, when you throe the ♡Q under the ♡K, declarer will simply exit with the ♡4 to your ♡6 – and endplay you just the same.

In the other room 6♡ was made. How about you? Was it a flat board, or did you scrape a win by 2 IMPs? The full hand was as shown.

```
                    ♠ A K Q 10 5
                    ♡ 10 2
                    ◊ J 10 7
                    ♣ J 6 5
   ♠ J 7 2                            ♠ 9 8 6 4 3
   ♡ Q 6 3        ┌─────────┐         ♡ J
   ◊ Q 6 5 4 3 2  │    N    │         ◊ 9
   ♣ 8            │ W     E │         ♣ K Q 10 9 7 2
                  │    S    │
                  └─────────┘
                    ♠ –
                    ♡ A K 9 8 7 5 4
                    ◊ A K 8
                    ♣ A 4 3
```

A Bidding Quiz by Andrew Kambites (page 149)

1) (a) 1♡. The *higher* of two five-card suits.

   (b) 1♡. Look for a major-suit fit before agreeing a minor.

   (c) 4♡. Before the opposition find they have a spade fit!

   (d) 1NT. This hand seems to be a misfit, so you should keep the bidding low. The trouble with 2♡ (or 2◊) is that you compel partner to rebid. If he rebids 2♠ you will have to pass, leaving him in a silly contract.

(2) (a) 1♡. It pays to get into the bidding at pairs. If you pass, and South plays in no-trumps, you can be sure that West will lead an unwelcome black-suit fourth-highest.

   (b) Pass. There are limits! If you overcall at the two-level, partner will expect more than this. Of course you cannot double and then remove 2♣ to 2◊, as this shows a single-suited hand *too strong* for an immediate 2◊ overcall.

   (c) 2♡. Don't sell out in the protective position. You know partner has some points!

   (d) Pass. Of course you want to compete in the protective seat, but ask yourself, 'Who has the spades?'

   If partner has spades, he must be very weak not to overcall 1◊ with 1♠. In that case, North–South surely have the majority of the points and can score much better in no-trumps than diamonds.

If North–South have the spades, they will have a higher-scoring part-score available in spades and, possessing the higher-ranking suit, they will outbid you in a competitive auction.

It is futile to compete protectively if all the evidence suggests that your opponents are in the wrong contract, and have the means to put this right if you give them a chance. Don't attack with a pea-shooter if the enemy has a machine-gun!

Freak Show by Dave Huggett (page 161)

The ♡Q was led against 6◊ and declarer ruffed, drew trumps, then played a small club to the Queen and King. A spade return from West was won in dummy, and after cashing a few superfluous trumps declarer played clubs from the top, eventually losing to the ♣10 on his right. He was even more dismayed to find that the spade finesse was right all along.

Declarer was guilty of not having tried to combine his chances. A better – and successful – way to have played clubs would have been to play low towards the Jack. If West goes in with the King, there are twelve top tricks; while, if he plays low, declarer can play a small one back to the ♣9, losing only when West started with ♣K–10–x–x or East has been very clever in withholding the King from ♣K–x–x–x. If East wins the first trick, then declarer has the luxury of later seeing if the clubs break and, if not, of taking the spade finesse The full hand was as shown.

```
                    ♠ A Q 6 3
                    ♡ K 6 5 4
                    ◊ A Q
                    ♣ J 6 5
    ♠ K 9 8 7          N          ♠ J 10 5 4
    ♡ Q J 10 7 3               ♡ A 9 8 2
    ◊ 9 5        W        E     ◊ 3
    ♣ K 2              S          ♣ 10 8 7 4
                    ♠ 2
                    ♡ –
                    ◊ K J 10 8 7 6 4 2
                    ♣ A Q 9 3
```

Acol Bidding Quiz by Amanda Hawthorn (page 173)

Deal 1: Dealer: East. N/S Vul.

						West	East
♠ 7 6 5 4 3			N		♠ A K Q 10 9		1♠
♡ 3	W			E	♡ 7 6 5	4♠	End
◇ Q J 10 9 8					◇ K 6		
♣ K 7			S		♣ 9 6 4		

West has the ideal hand for a pre-emptive jump to game. Surely North–South have a game in hearts – don't give them room to choose between playing their contract or doubling yours!

Deal 2: Dealer: East. Game All.

						West	East
♠ 3			N		♠ K Q 9 6 5 2		1♠
♡ A K 8 6 3					♡ 4 2	2♡	2♠
◇ A K 9 7 5	W			E	◇ Q J 4 3	3◇	4◇
♣ K 9			S		♣ A	4NT	5◇
						6◇	End

West must not force with 3♡ on the first round or the diamond fit will be missed. East is not strong enough to rebid 3◇, but after he has limited his hand with 2♠ he can freely raise 3◇ to 4◇. After the Blackwood enquiry has revealed East to have one Ace, West is happy to bid the slam.

Deal 3: Dealer: West. Game All.

						West	East
♠ A Q J			N		♠ 5 4 2	1◇	3◇
♡ A 10 5					♡ K J 8	3NT	End
◇ Q J 8 6	W			E	◇ K 10 9 2		
♣ A 8 5			S		♣ Q J 10		

East has a simple limit-raise to 3◇ – a 2NT bid 'to show point count' would be unwise with the spades wide open. With his balanced hand, West rather naturally settles for a nine-trick game rather than an eleven-trick one.

A Problem for Improvers by Mike Whittaker (page 193)

♠ A J 10 6 4
♡ J 7
◊ J 7 4 2
♣ 9 8

♠ K Q 9 8 7 5 2
♡ A
◊ A K 5
♣ A Q

Provided West holds the ♡Q, South can guarantee the contract. After winning the lead and drawing the outstanding trump, South cashes the ◊A and ◊K. A spade to dummy's ♠A is followed by the ♡J on which South discards his third diamond.

West wins, but must concede a twelfth trick. A club gives two club tricks, a heart gives a ruff-and-discard, and a diamond gives, or sets up, a diamond trick.

Third and Last by Richard Wheen (page 207)

It is possible that there is more than one solution to this problem, but here is mine anyway:

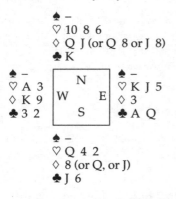

♠ –
♡ 10 8 6
◊ Q J (or Q 8 or J 8)
♣ K

♠ –
♡ A 3
◊ K 9
♣ 3 2

♠ –
♡ K J 5
◊ 3
♣ A Q

♠ –
♡ Q 4 2
◊ 8 (or Q, or J)
♣ J 6

The way the play goes with this layout is like this: West leads a club, covered by North's ♣K and won with the ♣A by East, who then leads the ♡J. South must cover with the ♡Q to prevent East–West immediately adding three heart tricks to the diamond and two club tricks to which they are entitled. West wins with the ♡A, and leads a club or a heart to East's honour card (if this is a heart then East goes on to cash his ♣Q). The club lead squeezes North, who must relinquish his guard in either hearts or diamonds, thereby enabling East–West to win the remaining tricks.

Note that the clubs and hearts must be arranged exactly as shown. If the heart spots are arranged differently, the solution will not work as North will be able to unblock his hearts so as to leave South still controlling the third round.

WHO'S WHO

Gustavu Aglione (a pseudonym) plays bridge in the Netherlands.

Simon Ainger writes for BRIDGE PLUS and *Country Magazine*.

Stein Aker plays bridge in Norway.

Jimmy Allan has contributed to most major international magazines.

Ulrich Auhagen is one of Germany's leading bridge theorists.

John Barr plays in Berkshire.

John Beard is the author of several bridge books and runs *JB Courses*. Bridge Holiday enquiries are welcome on 0752 550838.

David Barnes plays bridge in Berkshire.

Guy Beresiner and *InterCol Playing Cards* cater for all bridge clubs' card requirements (telephone: 081 343 7917).

David Bird is best known for his stories about the monks at the St Titus Monastery. The Gollancz Master Bridge Series have published four compilations of Abbot stories, by Terence Reese and David Bird: *Miracles of Cardplay*, *Doubled and Venerable*, *Unholy Tricks*, and *Cardinal Sins*.

Jane Bodin is the proprietor of Wolverhampton Bridge Club, 86 Tettenhall Road, Wolverhampton WV1 4TF (telephone: 0902 20927).

Raymond Brock is a British International and the General Manager of the English Bridge Union.

David Burn is the Chairman of the EBU's Law & Ethics Committee, and the author of *How to Survive Your First Bridge Tournament*.

Su Burn is an English International.

Stephen Cashmore writes for BRIDGE PLUS.

Pat Cotter is the *Financial Times* Bridge Columnist.

Eric Crowhurst is the author of *Precision Bidding in Acol*, *Acol in Competition*, and (together with Andrew Kambites) *Understanding Acol*.

Stephen Dabby plays bridge in London.

Neven Deleva is a former Bulgarian European Champion, a bridge teacher, writer, and professional player.

Maureen Dennison is a British International and a regular contributor to several bridge magazines.

Roy Dempster is the Tournament Director for *Five Star Bridge*. Bridge Holiday enquiries are welcome on 08243 530.

Albert Dorrington is the author of *Bidding for Social Bridge Players*.

David Ellis plays bridge in West Sussex.

Ruth Edmonson is the Project Manager of the *Bridge Club Guide to Britain and Ireland*.

Alasdair Forbes is the Editor of the *Scottish Bridge Union News magazine*.

Tony Forrester is *The Daily Telegraph* Bridge Columnist, a former European Champion, and the author of *Secrets of Success*.

G C H Fox, formerly *The Daily Telegraph* Bridge Columnist, is an internationally acclaimed author and teacher.

Tony Gordon writes for BRIDGE PLUS.

Alan Grace plays bridge in Surrey.

Nigel Guthrie writes for BRIDGE PLUS.

Jason Hackett is a British Junior International.

Paul Hackett writes for several international magazines.

Geoff Halliday plays bridge in North Yorkshire.

David Hamilton is a Welsh International and the *Western Daily Press* Bridge Columnist.

Peter Hawkes is a Camrose triallist and Spring Foursomes winner.

Tony Haworth is a former Chairman of the Welsh Bridge Union.

Amanda Hawthorn is the author, together with Rhoda Lederer, of *Improve Your Bridge the Lederer Way*.

Ken Hayton plays bridge in Yorkshire.

Ron Heath is an EBU Tournament Director.

Graham Hedley plays bridge in Hampshire.

Martin Hoffman is a bridge professional and writer, author of *More Tales from Hoffman*.

Mark Horton is an English International who is the Advertising Manager of *International Popular Bridge Monthly*, and the author of *Step by Step Guide to Defensive Signals*.

Sally Horton is a British International, former World Champion, and the author of *Double Trouble*.

Dave Huggett is one of England's leading players and a regular contributor to BRIDGE PLUS.

Pat Husband is the Manager of the English Bridge Union Teachers' Association.

Sam Jones plays bridge in Belfast.

Stuart Jones plays bridge in the Midlands.

Patrick Jourdain is the Bridge Correspondent of *The Daily Telegraph* and Principal of the Cardiff School of Bridge.

Andrew Kambites is the author of several books, amongst which are *Understanding Acol* (written together with Eric Crowhurst) and *Defensive Skills For You*.

Richard Kent plays bridge in Alicante.

Chris Kinloch plays in the South of England.

Jack Kroes is a Dutch bridge journalist.

Norman Mackenzie plays bridge in Aberdeen.

Bernard Magee writes for several bridge magazines.

Zia Mahmood is a Pakistani International and the author of *Bridge My Way*.

Morag Malcolm is a Scottish International.

Jeff Morris is the proprietor of Manchester Bridge Club, 30 Palatine Road, Manchester M20 9JJ (telephone: 061 445 3712).

Jim Mulcahy welcomes Bridge Stationery enquiries at *Top Table* and *A.L. Fleming* (telephone: 081 313 0350).

Svend Novrup is the Bridge Columnist of Danish national newspaper *Politiken*.

David Parry, a Grand Master, teaches bridge in Central London and Hampshire/West Sussex (telephone/fax: 081 749 4352 or 0705 631725).

Tony Parkinson plays bridge in Berkshire.

Derek Patterson and **Mark Howarth** are the authors of *Pre-empt*, the first volume in the *Alert!* series published by A.L. Fleming.

Queenie Penguin writes for BRIDGE PLUS.

Arthur Perelman played in North Yorkshire. The article on pp 174–175 was the last he wrote for BRIDGE PLUS before his death.

David Perkins plays bridge in Buckinghamshire.

Ron Pick is an EBU Tournament Director and writes regularly for BRIDGE PLUS.

Colin Porch is an EBU Tournament Director.

David Poriss is a 1992 Bols Tips finalist and teaches bridge in Connecticut.

Max Powell is a Tournament Director and former Chairman of the Welsh Bridge Union.

Don Putnam compiles crossword puzzles for *The Guardian*, and plays bridge in Lancashire.

Tony Richards plays bridge in Surrey.

Barry Rigal is *The Times* Bridge Correspondent and the author of *Test Your Bidding Judgement*.

Andrew Robson is a former European and Junior World Champion, author (together with Oliver Segal) of *Partnership Bidding at Bridge – The Contested Auction*, and the manager of The Acol Club, London (telephone: 071 624 7407).

Andy Roland welcomes enquiries on Bridge Computers at *Contemporary Games* (telephone 081 577 1700).

Danny Roth's latest books are *The Expert Advancer* and *The Expert Club Player*.

Bob Rowlands is one of England's leading players and a regular contributor to several bridge magazines.

Peter Rowlett teaches bridge in Northamptonshire.

Alec Salisbury is the EBU Youth Officer in charge of Schools Bridge.

Harold Schogger is the proprietor of 77 Bridge Club, 81a Brent Street, London NW4 2DY (telephone: 081 202 4718).

Brian Senior is the Executive Editor of *International Popular Bridge Monthly* and the author of *Clever Bridge Tricks*.

P F Saunders' latest book is *Bridge with my Granddaughter*.

Erwin Schon plays bridge in Kent.

Malcolm Simpson plays and teaches bridge in Oxfordshire.

Tony Sowter is a British International and the Managing Editor of *International Popular Bridge Monthly*.

Bill Starr is the Tournament Director at the Corbett Arms Hotel and Bridge Club (telephone: 0654 710264).

Peter Stocken is the Vice-Chairman of the English Bridge Union.

Mike Swanson is the Tournament Director for *Diamond Bridge*. Bridge Holiday enquiries are welcome on 0922 26017.

Kitty Teltscher plays bridge in London.

Tom Townsend is a British Junior International.

Roger Trowell plays bridge in Berkshire.

Wendy Wensum (alias Nigel Block) plays bridge in Norfolk.

Richard Wheen is the author (together with Nicola Smith) of *Bridge Player Galactica*.

Mike Whittaker is the author of *Bridgewise*.

N E Wood (a pseudonym) plays all his bridge(s) in South Africa.

Elena Jeronimidis is the Bridge Columnist of *Teletext on 4* and the Editor of BRIDGE PLUS, the monthly magazine available by subscription from P O Box 384, Reading RG1 5YP (telephone/fax: 0822 833080).